my **revisi⏻n** notes

A2 Edexcel History
A WORLD DIVIDED
SUPERPOWER RELATIONS, 1944–90

WITHDRAWN

Les Barker
Robin Bunce
Laura Gallagher

WITHDRAWN

The publishers would like to thank the following for permission to reproduce copyright material:

Acknowledgements

Archie Brown: extracts from 'The Gorbachev revolution and the end of the Cold War' and **Beth Fisher**, extracts from 'US foreign policy under Reagan and Bush' from The Cambridge History of the Cold War, edited by Melvyn P Leffler and Odd Arne Westad (Cambridge University Press, 2010); **John Lewis Gaddis**: extracts from The Cold War (Penguin Books, 2005); **Richard Haslam**: extracts from Russia's Cold War: From October Revolution to the Fall of the Wall (Yale University Press, 2011); **Robert J McMahon**: extracts from The Cold War (Oxford University Press, 2003); **Geoffrey Roberts**: extracts from Stalin's Wars: From World War to Cold War, 1939-1953 (Yale University Press, 2007).

Every effort has been made to trace all copyright holders, but if any have been inadvertently overlooked the Publishers will be pleased to make the necessary arrangements at the first opportunity.

Although every effort has been made to ensure that website addresses are correct at time of going to press, Hodder Education cannot be held responsible for the content of any website mentioned in this book. It is sometimes possible to find a relocated web page by typing in the address of the home page for a website in the URL window of your browser.

Hachette UK's policy is to use papers that are natural, renewable and recyclable products and made from wood grown in sustainable forests. The logging and manufacturing processes are expected to conform to the environmental regulations of the country of origin.

Orders: please contact Bookpoint Ltd, 130 Milton Park, Abingdon, Oxon OX14 4SB.
Telephone: +44 (0)1235 827720. Fax: +44 (0)1235 400454. Lines are open 9.00a.m.–5.00p.m., Monday to Saturday, with a 24-hour message answering service. Visit our website at www.hoddereducation.co.uk.

© Les Barker, Robin Bunce and Laura Gallagher 2013
First published in 2013 by
Hodder Education,
an Hachette UK company
338 Euston Road
London NW1 3BH

Impression number 10 9 8 7 6 5 4 3 2 1
Year 2017 2016 2015 2014 2013

Cover photo © Martin Konz/Alamy

Typeset in 11/13 Stempel Schneidler Std-Light by Datapage (India) Pvt. Ltd.
Artwork by Datapage
Printed and bound in Spain

A catalogue record for this title is available from the British Library

ISBN 978 1 444 177701

Contents

Introduction

About Unit 3

Unit 3 is worth 60 per cent of your A2 level. It requires detailed knowledge of a historical period and the ability to explore and analyse the interpretations of historians. Overall, 34 per cent of the marks available are awarded for source analysis (Assessment Objective 2, or AO2), and 66 per cent for using own knowledge to form an explanation (Assessment Objective 1, or AO1).

In the exam, you are required to answer one question with two parts. Part (a) is worth 30 marks and Part (b) is worth 40 marks. It is advisable to spend approximately two-fifths of your time in the exam on Part (a) and the remaining three-fifths on Part (b). There will be a choice of two questions in both Part (a) and Part (b). You must answer one Part (a) and one Part (b) question.

Part (a) focuses on AO1. It will test your ability to:

- ■ select information that focuses on the question
- ■ organise this information to provide an answer to the question
- ■ show range and depth in the examples you provide
- ■ analyse the significance of the information used to reach an overall judgement.

Part (b) focuses on both AO1 and AO2. It will test your ability to:

- ■ select information that focuses on the question
- ■ organise this information to provide an answer to the question
- ■ identify the interpretations provided by the sources
- ■ weigh the interpretations of the sources, and integrate these interpretations with evidence from your own knowledge to reach an overall judgement.

A World Divided: Superpower Relations, 1944–90

The exam board specifies that students should study four general areas, which will be examined in Part (a):

1. The post-Stalin thaw and the bid for peaceful coexistence
2. The arms race, 1949–1963

3. Sino-Soviet relations, 1949–1976
4. *Détente*, 1969–1980

In addition, the exam board specifies that students should study two historical controversies, which will be examined in Part (b):

1. Why did the Cold War between the superpowers emerge in the years to 1953?
2. Why did the Cold War come to an end in the 1980s?

How to use this book

This book has been designed to help you to develop the knowledge and skills necessary to succeed in this exam. The book is divided into six sections – one for each general area of the course. Each section is made up of a series of topics organised into double-page spreads. On the left-hand page, you will find a summary of the key content you need to learn. Words in bold in the key content are defined in the glossary. On the right-hand page, you will find exam-focused activities. Together, these two strands of the book will take you through the knowledge and skills essential for exam success.

There are three levels of exam-focused activities.

- ■ Band 1 activities are designed to develop the foundational skills needed to pass the exam.
- ■ Band 2 activities are designed to build on the skills developed in Band 1 activities and to help you achieve a C grade.
- ■ Band 3 activities are designed to enable you to access the highest grades.

Each section ends with an exam-style question and a model A grade answer with commentary. This should give you guidance on what is required to achieve the top grades.

Section 1: Why did the Cold War between the superpowers emerge in the years to 1953?

Ideology and the Cold War

The Second World War led to the decline of the big empires and the rise of two **superpowers**: the US and the **Soviet Union**. The superpowers were divided ideologically; they had competing strategic interests, and there was a legacy of mistrust between their leaders.

Ideological competition

These two superpowers represented competing economic and political systems:

	Political system	Economic system	World view
US	Democracy: • Free and regular elections allow the people to choose a government from competing political parties. • Individual rights are protected by law.	**Capitalism:** • The government plays a small role in the economy. • Goods and services are provided by privately owned businesses.	Free trade: • Peace and prosperity are created through free trade between nations.
Soviet Union	Single party government: • The Communist Party is the only legal party and dominates the government. • Political freedom is restricted; citizens have very limited rights to express themselves or to protest.	State **Socialism** (planned economy): • The government controls the country's economy. • Goods and services are produced according to a government plan and sold at fixed prices.	World revolution: • Freedom and equality can only be achieved through a world revolution that replaces capitalism with **communism**.

Evidence of ideological conflict

Ideology seems to have played a role in East–West relations prior to the **Cold War**:

- British and US troops intervened in the **Russian Civil War** (1918–1920) in an attempt to overthrow the communist government.
- Western powers refused to recognise the Soviet Union as a legitimate state and admit it to the **League of Nations** following the First World War.
- During the US '**Red Scare**' of 1919, US government officials attempted to hunt down and expel **left-wing** radicals from the US.
- The Soviet Union's foreign policy from 1917 to 1941 was largely based on the assumption that Western capitalist powers were hostile to communism.
- Soviet propaganda from 1917 to 1941 was consistently anti-capitalist.

Key interpretation: ideological confrontation

One explanation of the origins of the Cold War focuses on the ideological confrontation between the US and the Soviet Union. According to this interpretation, the Cold War was an inevitable conflict as capitalism and communism were fundamentally antagonistic to one another. **Marxism-Leninism**, the official ideology of the Soviet Union, explicitly committed the Communist Party to work for a world revolution to overthrow capitalism. Equally, US economic success depended on free trade with the whole of the industrialised world, while the Soviet economic system was based on a rejection of free markets and free trade.
This interpretation is useful as it explains East–West conflict prior to the Cold War, such as the US and British attempt to overthrow the communist government of Russia during the Russian Civil War of 1918 to 1920. However, it assumes that the leaders of the two superpowers were entirely guided by their ideologies, when in reality they were prepared to act more pragmatically.

Below are a sample Part (b) exam-style question and the three sources referred to in the question. In one colour, draw links between the sources to show ways in which they agree about the development of the Cold War. In another colour, draw links between the sources to show ways in which they disagree.

Use Sources 1, 2 and 3 and your own knowledge.

How far do you agree with the view that the development of the Cold War in the years 1945–1953 was primarily a result of ideological conflict between the superpowers?

SOURCE 1

(From Arthur Schlesinger, 'Origins of the Cold War' in Foreign Affairs 46, *published 1967)*

The Cold War could have been avoided only if the Soviet Union had not been possessed by convictions both of the infallibility of the Communist word and of the inevitability of a Communist world. These convictions transformed a stalemate between national states into a religious war, a tragedy of possibility into one of necessity. One might wish that America had preserved the poise and proportion of the first years of the Cold War and had not in time succumbed to its own forms of self-righteousness. But the most rational of American policies could hardly have averted the Cold War.

SOURCE 2

(From Jonathan Haslam in Russia's Cold War: From October Revolution to the Fall of the Wall, *published 2011)*

The Cold War did not, of course, burst in suddenly on an entirely harmonious world. The conflict had deep-seated ideological foundations that outlasted leaders who differed in the degree of attachment to fundamental principle in the conduct of foreign policy. On the grand scale of history the Cold War stemmed directly from a thoroughgoing revolt against Western values, a wholesale rejection of an entire way of life and its economic underpinnings, and the substitution of something new and entirely alien in terms of culture and experience. That revolt began with the [Russian] Revolution in 1917.

SOURCE 3

(From John Lewis Gaddis in The United States and the Origins of the Cold War, *published 1972)*

The Cold War grew out of complicated interaction of external and internal developments inside both the United States and the Soviet Union. The external situation – circumstances beyond the control of either power – left Americans and Russians facing one another across prostrated Europe at the end of World War II. Internal influences in the Soviet Union – the search for security, the role of ideology, massive postwar construction needs, the personality of Stalin – together with those in the United States – the ideal of self-determination, fear of communism, the illusion of total power fostered by American economic strength and the atomic bomb – made the resulting confrontation a hostile one. Leaders of both superpowers sought peace, but in doing so yielded to considerations which, while they did not precipitate war, made a resolution of differences impossible.

The Second World War and the two superpowers

In spite of their ideological differences, the US and the Soviet Union were part of a military alliance, which also comprised Britain, during the Second World War. This was known as the Grand Alliance and was formed to combat the **Axis Powers**. The war's impact was global. It led to the decline of the big French and British Empires and the rise of two very different superpowers: the US and the Soviet Union.

The US in 1945

Harry Truman became US president in April 1945. He presided over the greatest military and economic power the world had ever known.

- War production had created an economic boom doubling the US's **GDP** between 1941 and 1945.
- The US had half of the world's manufacturing capacity, three times that of the Soviet Union.
- The US had developed the **atomic bomb**, which gave it an overwhelming military supremacy.
- The **Bretton Woods Conference** established the dollar as the world's principal trading currency.

However, there were doubts and fears. The political leadership had been deeply scarred by the impact of the **Great Depression** and felt it was vital that its policies stimulated prosperity for the world, but especially for the US. There was a fear that communist ideology might have great appeal for millions who lived in daily poverty.

The Soviet Union in 1945

For the Soviet Union the picture was very different. The war had led to:

- the death of 27 million people
- the destruction of 1700 cities and towns
- the destruction of much of the country's industrial and agricultural infrastructure.

However, the Soviet Union had several advantages:

- It had played the biggest role in defeating Hitler and therefore was guaranteed a major role in determining the post-war settlement.
- It had the largest army in the world. By 1945 the Russian army comprised 11 million men.
- Between 1945 and 1953 the Soviet economy was the fastest growing economy in the world.

Stalin's objectives for the post-war world

Stalin wanted to guarantee the security of the Soviet Union from foreign invasion. Initially he spoke of **peaceful coexistence** with the West. At the same time, Stalin was willing to guarantee Soviet security by:

- ensuring Soviet dominance over Poland, which had been an avenue into Russia for invaders
- keeping Germany weak
- extending Soviet territory and influence in Eastern Europe.

Key interpretation: Stalin's aggression

Some historians argue that Stalin's policies in the years following the Second World War were the main cause of the Cold War. From this point of view, Soviet determination to create a **sphere of influence** in Eastern Europe can be interpreted as a sign of Soviet aggression. Further evidence for this view comes from Stalin's refusal to tolerate opposition parties and his willingness to eliminate leaders such as Masaryk in Czechoslovakia (see page 12). His actions over Berlin in 1948 (see page 16) can also be regarded as an attempt to coerce the West into accepting the Soviet plan for the future of Germany. According to this interpretation, the US played a largely reactive role and it was the aggressive nature of Soviet foreign policy that brought about the Cold War. Notably, this interpretation overlooks Stalin's commitment, until 1947, to peaceful coexistence between the superpowers.

Add own knowledge

Below are a sample Part (b) exam-style question and the three sources referred to in the question. In one colour, draw links between the sources to show ways in which they agree about the importance of Soviet aggression as a factor in the development of the Cold War. In another colour, draw links between the sources to show ways in which they disagree. Around the edge of the sources, write relevant own knowledge. Again, draw links to show the ways in which this agrees or disagrees with the sources.

Use Sources 1, 2 and 3 and your own knowledge.

How far do you agree with the view that Soviet aggression accounts for the development of the Cold War in the years 1945–1953?

SOURCE 1

(From Michael Lind in The American Way of Strategy, *published 2006)*

The Cold War began in the late 1940s when Joseph Stalin refused to remove the Russian army from eastern Europe, imposed communist regimes on the region, began a massive arms buildup, and sponsored communist revolutions throughout the world. The Cold War began in Europe and ended in Europe. It was caused by Soviet aggression and it ended with Soviet surrender.

SOURCE 2

(From Martin McCauley in Origins of the Cold War 1941–49, *published 2008)*

Stalin must bear much of the blame for the Cold War because he had it within his power in 1945 to fashion a working relationship with the United States. Neither Stalin nor Truman wanted a Cold War. Perhaps in 1945 both the Soviet and American leaders were too confident that their own system would eventually win. However, in the short term, because of the depredations of war, both felt nervous about the other's ability to steal a march on them.

SOURCE 3

(From Robert J McMahon in The Cold War, *published 2003)*

For all his ruthlessness and paranoia, and for all his cruelty towards his own people, Stalin pursued a generally cautious, circumspect foreign policy, seeking always to balance opportunity with risk. The Russian dictator invariably calculated with great care the prevailing 'correlation of forces'. He [had] a realist's respect for the superior military and industrial power possessed by the United States and often sought the proverbial half a loaf when pursuit of a full loaf seemed likely to generate resistance. The needs of the Soviet state, which always took precedence for Stalin over the desire to spread communism, dictated a policy that mixed opportunism with caution and an inclination to compromise, not a strategy of aggressive expansion.

Shaping the post-war world

Between 1943 and 1945, representatives of the US, the Soviet Union and Britain met four times to agree a common approach to rebuilding Europe. The meetings left important issues unresolved, issues that became fundamental in the early years of the Cold War.

Tehran and Moscow

Leaders of the allied nations met in Tehran in 1943 and Moscow in 1944. Over the course of these meetings they discussed post-war spheres of influence. At the Moscow conference **Churchill** and Stalin agreed that:

- Britain would be allowed to station troops in Greece
- the Soviet Union would retain troops in Romania, Bulgaria and Hungary.

The Yalta Conference, February 1945

The leaders went into the conference with different priorities.

- Churchill was anxious that the pro-Western Polish government, in exile in London, should be returned to power in Poland.
- Stalin was concerned to ensure that Germany did not re-emerge as a military power and that Poland was part of the Soviet sphere of influence.
- **Roosevelt** wanted acceptance of the **United Nations** and a Soviet agreement to enter the war against Japan.

The US and Britain accepted Soviet demands. In return, Stalin agreed to the establishment of the UN after the Soviet Union's right of **veto** was confirmed, and said the Soviet Union would enter the war against Japan when it had completed its campaign in Europe.

The Potsdam Conference, July 1945

The Potsdam Agreement divided Germany temporarily into four zones, each controlled by one of the victorious **Allies**. It also established new borders for Germany and Poland that suited Stalin, although it became clear that Stalin would not accept a return of the **Polish government in exile**. Key questions over the future of Germany and the extent of Soviet control over Eastern Europe remained unresolved. Nonetheless, the three powers agreed that no decision could be made regarding the future of Germany without trilateral agreement.

Key interpretation: great power rivalry

Some historians argue that the Cold War was a continuation of existing trends in the relations between the world's great powers. For example, some argue that the Soviet Union simply continued the Russian tradition of empire building. Similarly, it can also be argued that US policy in Asia, notably its increasing links with Japan, was a continuation of the **open door policy** for expansion in the nineteenth century. Historians who claim that the Cold War emerged from great power rivalry play down ideological divisions, explaining the Cold War as a clash of two great powers who sought to extend their global influence.

Evidence to support this interpretation can be found in the period at the end of the Second World War. At this time Stalin was determined to consolidate his war gains and achieve international recognition for the Soviet domination of Eastern Europe. Similarly, the Western powers felt it vital, both politically and economically, to safeguard the areas within their spheres of influence. It could be argued that this rivalry was evident in the negotiations at Tehran, Yalta and Potsdam. Indeed, some historians argue that the Yalta settlement, which recognised the reality of Soviet dominance in Eastern Europe, laid the foundations of a divided Europe.

Below are a sample Part (b) exam-style question and the three sources referred to in the question. Each source offers an interpretation of the issue raised by the question. Below each source, summarise the interpretation offered by the source.

Use Sources 1, 2 and 3 and your own knowledge.

How far do you agree with the view that the development of the Cold War in the years 1945–1953 was primarily due to rivalry between the great world powers?

SOURCE 1

(From William Appleman Williams in The Vision of Omnipotence and America's Role in the Cold War, *published 1971)*

A nation with the great power enjoyed by the United States between 1944 and 1962 cannot claim that it has been *forced* to follow a certain approach or policy. Yet that is the American claim in the early years of the Cold War. The United States used its preponderance of power wholly within the assumptions and the tradition of the strategy of the Open Door Policy. The United States never offered the Soviet Union a settlement based on other, less grandiose, terms. The popular idea that Soviet leaders emerged from the war ready to do aggressive battle against the United States is simply not borne out by the evidence.

SOURCE 2

(From RC Raack in Stalin's Drive to the West, 1938–1945, *published 2005)*

At Potsdam, Harry Truman grew increasingly impatient. His predecessor's faith in Stalin had helped to create the situation he faced in the summer of 1945. But it became quite evident in the course of the Potsdam Conference that he had no real alternative except to abandon that faith, to deal with Stalin on his terms, those of confrontation.

The Western governments, for good reason, had uneasily watched Stalin's carrying out of the Yalta agreements on the Polish government issue. When the subject of Poland's borders came up again at the Potsdam Conference, Western reaction to Stalin's arrogance was almost palpable. At Potsdam the Western leaders for the first time drew important limits to prevent Soviet expansion. Potsdam marked the first major diplomatic stage in the development of the Cold War as a conflict.

SOURCE 3

(From Fraser J Harbutt in Yalta 1945: Europe and America at the Crossroads, *published 2010)*

Up to the beginning of 1945, it was almost universally assumed that the postwar world would [comprise] a battered but still autonomous Anglo-Soviet-led Europe looking across the Atlantic to a benevolent, financially supportive but still politically distant United States. In fact, of course, things turned out very differently. At some point – in and around the time of the Yalta conference – the political situation was quite suddenly transformed. The Europe / America framework began to break down, and the East / West configuration came into view. Many people look back to Yalta to explain the origins of the Cold War.

Growing tension: Kennan, Novikov and Churchill

Revised

At the end of 1945, the two new superpowers were technically allies. However, during 1946 the relationship between them became increasingly strained. Two telegrams, sent by Kennan and Novikov, shed light on the attitudes of senior officials on both sides.

The Kennan telegram, February 1946

George Kennan was a US diplomat who had been based in the Soviet Union since 1933. In February 1946, Kennan sent a telegram to the US government alerting them to his fears that the Soviet Union was preparing for world domination. Essentially, Kennan predicted a life and death struggle between democracy and communism. Kennan advised that, 'The main element of United States policy towards the Soviet Union must be of firm and vigilant **containment**'. Containment became the defining feature of US policy in the first years of the Cold War.

The Novikov telegram, September 1946

Later in the year, NV Novikov, the Soviet ambassador to the US, sent a telegram to Moscow, which summed up his views. We know that Stalin studied this document closely. He expressed his concerns about the way in which the US was using its wealth to gain influence around the world. He argued that the US was beginning to act like an **imperialist** power. He argued that the expansion of the network of US military bases was a sign that the US government was planning 'global domination'.

Churchill, Stalin and the 'Iron Curtain'

In March 1946 Churchill spoke at Westminster College, Fulton, Missouri. This speech emphasised the bitter divisions that existed between the rival power blocs in Europe. He likened these divisions to an 'iron curtain'. Stalin responded by branding Churchill a warmonger.

Superpower relations at the end of 1946

By the end of 1946, it was clear that trust had broken down between the US and the Soviet Union. Both sides were convinced that the other was plotting world domination. Therefore, by the end of 1946 the Grand Alliance was essentially at an end. However, the fact that senior diplomats were still taking part in regular **bilateral** negotiations indicates that the superpowers were not yet in a state of Cold War.

Key interpretation: mutual misconceptions

Some historians have suggested that the Cold War came about due to mutual misconceptions and the different perspectives of the two superpowers. According to this interpretation, both superpowers were motivated by the desire to protect their own interests. However, these actions were misinterpreted as aggressive policies designed to expand their global influence. For example, actions that Soviet leaders perceived as legitimate to safeguard their own security, such as the **Stalinisation** of Eastern Europe (see page 12), were interpreted by US leaders as indicative of a desire to dominate. Similarly, Western initiatives, such as the introduction of a new currency into the Western zone of Germany (see page 16), were viewed as provocative by Soviet leaders. In this sense, the Cold War developed due to a series of misunderstandings and overreactions.

Contrasting interpretations

Below are three sources offering interpretations regarding the reasons for the development of the Cold War in the period 1945–1953. Identify the interpretation offered in each source and complete the table below, indicating how far the sources agree with each other, and explaining your answer.

	Extent of agreement	Justification
Sources 1 and 2		
Sources 1 and 3		
Sources 2 and 3		

SOURCE 1

(From Charles S Maier in The Origins of the Cold War and Contemporary Europe, *published 1978)*

By late 1945 the United States and Russia each felt itself to be at a competitive disadvantage in key disputes. Each felt that the other, being ahead, could best afford to make initial concessions, while gestures on its part would entail disproportionate or unilateral sacrifice. Perhaps more far-sighted leaders could have sought different outcomes, but there were pressures on all policy makers to take decisions that would harden conflict rather than alleviate it.

SOURCE 2

(From Mike Sewell in The Cold War, *published 2002)*

During 1946 Soviet relations with its wartime allies grew increasingly fraught. Old suspicions were revitalised in disagreements over the future of Europe. Competition and rivalry bedevilled day-to-day relations in Germany and Austria. Efforts to organise governments friendly to the Soviet Union in the Balkans and eastern Europe contributed to the deterioration of Western impressions of Stalin's ambitions. On the Soviet side, memories of the years before 1941 and conduct in the liberated lands contributed to policies that were not necessarily designed to alienate the West but frequently had the effect of doing so. Those who did not wish to see co-operation continue were gaining the upper hand in most major capitals.

SOURCE 3

(From Melvyn P Leffler in The Origins of the Cold War: An International History, *published 2005)*

In the frightening postwar environment American assessments of Soviet long-term intentions were transformed. Spurred by the 'long telegram' written by George F Kennan, it soon became commonplace for policymakers, military officials, and intelligence analysts to state that the ultimate aim of Soviet foreign policy was Russian domination of a Communist world.

Yet these assessments did not seriously grapple with contradictory evidence. They disregarded numerous signs of Soviet weaknesses. In October 1947 the Joint Intelligence Committee forecast a Soviet army troop strength during 1948 and 1949 of less than 2 million men. Other reports dealt with the inadequacies of Soviet transportation. Assessments of the Soviet economy revealed persistent problems likely to restrict Soviet adventurism.

The Truman doctrine and the Marshall Plan

In many ways, 1947 was a turning point in superpower relations. The significant change occurred when Truman set out his approach to superpower relations in the Truman doctrine.

The Truman doctrine, March 1947

Truman set out his position in a speech to **Congress** in March 1947. He committed the US to provide military and economic resources to stop the spread of communism. This policy became known as 'containment'. Soviet leaders responded by establishing **Cominform** to ensure Soviet control of its **satellite states**.

The Stalinisation of Eastern Europe

In the years 1947–1949, Cominform was successful in Stalinising Eastern Europe. Through rigged elections and the sponsorship of coups, Cominform created one-party dictatorships, mirroring Stalin's model of government. Examples are shown in the table below.

Country	Date of Stalinisation	Method used
Hungary	1947	Elections rigged to ensure communist victory.
Czechoslovakia	1948	Staged a coup to overthrow the elected government and replace it with a communist government. In addition, Foreign Minister Jan Masaryk was murdered.

By 1949, the majority of Eastern European states had been reduced to Soviet satellite states.

The Marshall Plan, June 1947

The Marshall Plan was an aid package designed to provide US money to promote economic recovery in Europe. Truman hoped that economic recovery in Europe would lead to increased trade with the US and sustained economic growth. He also hoped that Marshall Aid would tie European nations into a relationship with the US. In order to receive Marshall Aid, European countries had to agree to free trade. The scale was huge: 13.7 billion dollars in cash and commodities between 1948 and 1952.

Reactions to the Marshall Plan

Stalin made it clear that the **Eastern bloc** would not accept what was termed '**dollar imperialism**'. Stalin established **Comecon** as a Soviet alternative to Marshall Aid. It was designed to facilitate economic co-operation across the Eastern bloc and therefore promote economic growth.

The significance of the Marshall Plan

- The Marshall Plan and Comecon led to the emergence of two economic areas in Europe, one sponsored by the US, the other by the Soviet Union.
- The Marshall Plan led to economic recovery of the Western zones of Germany. This, in turn, led to the creation of a stable West German state outside of the Soviet sphere of influence.

Key interpretation: US dollar diplomacy

Some historians argue that US economic interest was the main reason for the development of the Cold War. There are a variety of different interpretations that focus on US economic interests:

- Superpower conflict came about due to the US desire to have the dominant political and economic position in western Europe and Japan. Historians who believe this interpretation argue that the Marshall Plan was a form of 'dollar imperialism' as US economic aid was dependent on political compliance.
- The Cold War developed due to the concerns of US politicians who were determined to avoid a repeat of the Great Depression. Historians interpret Truman's desire to promote trade with Western Europe and Japan as an attempt to stimulate the US economy through trade.
- Truman encouraged superpower tensions in order to justify massive government spending on arms to stimulate the US economy.

Below is a source providing an interpretation regarding the reasons for the development of the Cold War. You must read the source, identify the interpretation offered by the source, and use your own knowledge to provide a counter-argument, challenging the interpretation offered by the source.

SOURCE 1

(From Joyce and Gabriel Kolko in The Limits of Power: The World and United States Foreign Policy, 1945–1954, *published 1972)*

Essentially, the United States' aim [after the Second World War] was to restructure the world so that American business could trade, operate, and profit without restrictions everywhere. On this there was absolute unanimity among American leaders, and it was around this core that they elaborated their policies and programmes. American business could operate only in a world composed of politically reliable and stable capitalist nations, and with free access to essential raw materials. Such a universal order precluded the Left from power, and necessitated conservative, ultimately subservient, political control throughout the globe.

Interpretation offered by the source:

_____

_____

Counter-argument:

_____

_____

_____

_____

🛈 Write the question   **ⓐ**

The source above (Source 1) and the following sources relate to key factors in the development of the Cold War in the period 1945–1953. Consider the first historical controversy the exam board specified – Why did the Cold War between the superpowers emerge in the years to 1953? – and review the topics you have revised so far. Having done this, write a Part (b) exam-style question using the sources.

SOURCE 2

(From Robert Dallek in The Lost Peace: Leadership in a Time of Horror and Hope, 1945–1953, *published 2010)*

In Moscow's view, forcing [Czechoslovakia] into the Soviet camp was a strictly defensive action. But Stalin should have understood that making Czechoslovakia a Soviet satellite was bound to stir war talk in Western Europe and the United States, where the 'Czech Coup' was only seen as an act of aggression reminiscent of Hitler's prewar actions. A cable from General Lucius Clay, the commanding US officer in Berlin, who had considered war unlikely with Russia 'for at least ten years,' now predicted that a conflict 'may come with dramatic suddenness.'

SOURCE 3

(From John Lewis Gaddis, 'Was the Truman Doctrine a Real Turning Point?' in Foreign Affairs 52, *published 1974)*

Despite the sweeping language of the Truman Doctrine, the actual policies which the Truman administration followed between 1947 and 1950 hardly justify description as an all-out effort to contain communism everywhere. Rather, the Administration appears to have been seeking a world in which several centres of power could exist, each exerting a restraining influence upon the other. Obviously the Korean War was the decisive event which destroyed this pleasing prospect. The real commitment to contain communism everywhere originated in the events surrounding the Korean War.

Use Sources 1, 2 and 3 and your own knowledge.

How far do you agree that _____

_____

Explain your answer, using Sources 1, 2 and 3 and your own knowledge of the issues related to this controversy.

The roots of conflict over Berlin

After the end of the war in 1945, the future of Germany became a major issue dividing East and West.

The Soviet perspective

Stalin regarded Germany with great suspicion and hostility. He was determined to safeguard the Soviet Union from a potential German invasion by preventing Germany re-emerging as a military and economic power.

The US perspective

The US believed that the punishment of Germany at the end of the First World War had created the conditions in which political extremism developed. They felt that the best guarantee for future peace and prosperity in Europe would be the development of a democratic Germany built on a strong industrial base. They also felt that the economic recovery of Europe depended on free trade between Germany and other European nations.

The division of Germany

At the end of the Second World War, Germany had been divided into four zones:

- British
- French
- US
- Soviet.

The division was intended to be a temporary measure as the Allies anticipated the creation of a united German government in the near future.

Berlin

Berlin was also divided between the four powers. However, its position 177 kilometres inside the Soviet zone made it a potential focus of tension.

Stalin's desire for reunification

The Soviet Union feared the unification of the three Western zones of Germany as they believed that a united Western Germany would be a military threat to Eastern Europe and Russia. Consequently, Stalin argued for a fully united and neutral Germany. This was unacceptable to the US, who feared that this state would be absorbed into the Soviet sphere of influence. The fears of the two sides endured, and manifested themselves in the proposals put forward in 1947.

Bizonia and Trizonia

At the Moscow meeting of March 1947 the four powers considered a proposal from the US for urgent **monetary reform** in Germany to stimulate industrial development. The Soviet representatives rejected this as they felt it would be a means through which the capitalist US could gain greater influence.

The US was frustrated by the Soviet response. Consequently, the US and Britain began to discuss political integration. Together, the British and US zones became known as Bizonia. In May 1948 France agreed to work with Britain and the US on German currency reform. In April 1949, the three Western powers agreed on political integration between the three zones, creating Trizonia.

Key interpretation: Stalin's personality

Some historians have focused on Stalin's personality as the main reason for the development of the Cold War. They point to his feelings of insecurity, his desire to dominate, and his willingness to do anything to safeguard the future of the Soviet Union as the key factor in superpower relations.

Evidence to support this view comes from documents that only became available to historians following the end of the Cold War. These include records of memos from senior Soviet ministers such as Maxim Litvinov, who commented that, 'There has been a return in Russia to the concept of security in terms of territory – the more you've got the safer you are'. Stalin's suspicions certainly played a role in his policy towards Berlin, as he believed that a resurgent Germany posed a significant threat to the security of the Soviet Union.

RAG – Rate the sources

Below are a sample Part (b) exam-style question and the sources referred to in the question. Read the question, study each source and, using three coloured pens, underline it in Red, Amber and Green to show:

Red: Counter-arguments and counter-evidence provided by the source
Amber: Evidence that supports the interpretation in the question
Green: The interpretation offered by the question

Use Sources 1, 2 and 3 and your own knowledge.

How far do you agree with the view that Stalin was primarily responsible for the development of the Cold War between the US and the Soviet Union in the years 1945–1953?

SOURCE 1

(From John Lewis Gaddis in We Now Know: Rethinking the Cold War, *published 1997)*

Would there have been a Cold War without Stalin? Perhaps. Nobody in history is indispensable. But Stalin had certain characteristics that set him off from all others in authority at the time the Cold War began. He alone pursued personal security by depriving everyone else of it: no Western leader relied on terror to the extent that he did. He alone saw war and revolution as acceptable means with which to pursue ultimate ends: no Western leader associated violence with progress to the extent that he did.

Did Stalin therefore seek a Cold War? The question is a little like asking: 'does a fish seek water?' Suspicion, distrust, and an abiding cynicism were not only his preferred but his necessary environment; he could not function apart from it.

SOURCE 2

(From Robert J McMahon in The Cold War, *published 2003)*

To deal with the threat of communism, the United States moved with dizzying speed during the first half of 1947 to implement a strategy aimed simultaneously at containing the Soviet Union and reducing the appeal of communism. What is particularly significant about the Truman Doctrine is the manner in which the American president chose to present his aid proposal. Truman was striving to build a public and Congressional consensus behind a more active American foreign policy – a policy that would be at once anti-Soviet and anti-communist. The Truman Doctrine thus amounted to a declaration of ideological Cold War along with a declaration of geopolitical Cold War.

SOURCE 3

(From Geoffrey Roberts in Stalin's Wars: From World War to Cold War, 1939–1953, *published 2007)*

In April 1947 Stalin gave a personal interview to Republican politician Harold Stassen. Stalin's mood was upbeat. He pointed out to Stassen that despite the differences in their economic systems the Soviet Union and the United States had co-operated during the war and there was no reason why they could not continue to do so in peacetime. Each side supported its own social system, Stalin told Stassen, and which was better would be decided by history. The interview represented a determined effort by Stalin to return to the spirit of the Grand Alliance.

Within a very short time, however, Stalin was to abandon active pursuit of peace with the west and embrace a cold war and policy that was almost the mirror image of the Truman doctrine. The key event in precipitating this change in policy was the Marshall Plan. For Stalin the Marshall Plan was the breaking point in postwar relations with the United States. It indicated that co-operation with the Americans was no longer possible without putting in jeopardy the Soviet sphere of influence in eastern Europe.

The Berlin Crisis, 1948–1949

Revised

During 1948 and 1949 there was a tense stand-off over Berlin. Soviet leaders blockaded West Berlin in an attempt to force the US to abandon its plans to divide Germany between east and west.

The causes of the Crisis

The US was frustrated by the Soviet response. Together, Britain and the US began to discuss political integration.

- In May 1947, the British and US zones became known as Bizonia.
- In March 1948, Bizonia joined with the French zone to create Trizonia.
- In May 1948, the three powers began work on German currency reform.

The Berlin Blockade, 1948

On 18 June the new currency was issued in the Western zones of Germany. Stalin aimed to force the Western powers to halt their reforms by blockading West Berlin. He ordered the closing of all travel links from Trizonia to West Berlin and cut the power supply.

The Western response

The Berlin Airlift

The US could not accept this situation as Berlin was of enormous strategic value. Consequently, on 26 June it launched Operation Vittles, in order to keep West Berlin supplied by air. The British started a similar operation codenamed Plainfare. These operations used US and British planes to transport supplies to West Berlin. By May 1949, 2.3 million tons of supplies had been flown into the city.

The nuclear option

In August 1948 the US deployed 60 B29 bombers to Britain. These planes could carry nuclear weapons and this move was clearly designed to increase the pressure on the Soviet Union.

The significance of the Berlin Crisis

On 12 May 1949 Stalin conceded that the blockade had failed and reopened the communications routes.

The Crisis was significant for the following reasons:

- It illustrated the resolve of the West to stand up to Soviet pressure in a peaceful manner.
- It was a propaganda disaster for the Soviet Union. The Crisis suggested that Stalin was prepared to starve 2 million people in order to achieve his **geopolitical** objectives.
- The Soviets failed in their objective of preventing the formal unification of the three Western zones of Germany, and the Federal Republic of Germany (West Germany) was established on 23 May 1949. In response, the Soviet zone declared itself an independent state named the German Democratic Republic (East Germany).
- The US agreed to guarantee the security of Western Europe and **NATO** was set up in April 1949.
- Its peaceful resolution demonstrated that neither side wanted to escalate the conflict. Neither side wanted to risk nuclear war.

Key interpretation: US aggression

Some historians have argued that the Cold War developed due to US determination to confront the Soviet Union. From this point of view, the Truman doctrine and the Marshall Plan, together with US leadership of NATO, can be seen as the US asserting its power against Soviet influence. Additionally, US deployment of B29 bombers in Europe during the 1948 Berlin Crisis can also be interpreted as evidence of US aggression.

The following sources relate to key factors in the development of the Cold War in the period 1945–1953. Consider the first historical controversy the exam board specified – Why did the Cold War between the superpowers emerge in the years to 1953? – and review the topics you have revised so far. Having done this, write a Part (b) exam-style question using the sources.

SOURCE 1

(From Walter LaFeber, Richard Polenberg and Nancy Woloch in The American Century: A History of the United States Since 1941, *published 2008)*

Put simply, Russia's attention focused on Eastern and Central Europe, while America, as a worldwide, expansive economic power, took the entire globe as its province – including the Soviet sphere. For these reasons, the Cold War erupted not over questions in the Americas, Asia, or even Western Europe. It broke out because of American demands in Eastern and Central Europe, that is, in the areas that the Russians were determined to dominate.

SOURCE 2

(From Melvyn P Leffler in The Origins of the Cold War: An International History, *published 2005)*

What is remarkable is that after 1946 the monumental losses [suffered by the Soviet Union in the Second World War] received so little attention when American defence analysts studied the motives and intentions of Soviet policy. Indeed, defence officials did little to analyse the threat perceived by the Soviets. Yet these same officials had absolutely no doubt that the wartime experiences and sacrifices of the United States, though much less devastating than those of Soviet Russia, entitled the United States to oversee the [reconstruction] of Germany, establish a balance of power in Europe, and militarily dominate the borders of Europe, thereby safeguarding American access to raw materials and control over all sea and air approaches to North America.

SOURCE 3

(From Steve Phillips in The Cold War, *published 2001)*

The sheer scale of Soviet losses in the war added to [Stalin's] sense of insecurity. The war had resulted in the deaths of over 20 million Soviet citizens, the highest of any of the countries involved in the war. In addition, there was an enormous economic cost, with over 25 million people left homeless and losses in factories and farms amounting to one-third of the country's wealth. The USSR was not only economically weak but also concerned about its military weakness given the development of the atomic bomb by the USA. The Americans, who saw no fighting on their own soil, failed to understand this Soviet obsession with security. To the USSR a buffer zone of satellite states in eastern Europe was essential and US foreign policy moves after 1945 seemed to confirm the West's determination to undermine communism.

Use Sources 1, 2 and 3 and your own knowledge.

How far do you agree that _____

_____

Explain your answer, using Sources 1, 2 and 3 and your own knowledge of the issues related to this controversy.

The Korean War, 1950–1953

The Korean War was a landmark in the development of the Cold War. It involved the first military conflict between the Western powers and a communist state.

Why Korea?

Following the Potsdam Conference, Korea was partitioned along the **38th Parallel**. The Soviet Union controlled the north, and the US the south. In 1948, the division was formalised, with the creation of **North and South Korea**. Kim Il Sung led communist North Korea and Syngman Rhee led the capitalist South.

The outbreak of war

Kim was determined to reunite the country under his leadership. He petitioned Stalin for help. In 1950 Stalin agreed because:

- in 1949 the Soviet Union had successfully tested an atomic bomb, ending the US's **nuclear monopoly**
- in 1949 Mao Zedong had established a communist regime in neighbouring China
- in early 1950, US Secretary of State Dean Acheson had given a speech which appeared to exclude South Korea from the US's Asian **'defensive perimeter'**
- in June 1950, the North Korean army invaded South Korea, supported by Soviet tanks and aircraft.

US intervention

Truman was under intense domestic political pressure. The China Lobby held Truman responsible for the 'loss' of China to communism. Additionally, US officials felt that a communist takeover of Korea threatened Japan, a country central to US strategy in Asia.

NSC-68 (1950)

NSC-68 was a secret document setting out US policy in the Cold War. It argued that the Soviet Union was seeking world domination, and therefore that the US needed to massively increase its defence spending and be ready to take on communism with military force. US intervention in Korea was the first sign that NSC-68 was being implemented.

Containment or rollback?

The US took the issue to the UN. The **UN Security Council** authorised military intervention to restore independence to the South. The Soviet Union was unable to veto this decision as it was boycotting the Security Council in protest at the UN's refusal to admit communist China as a member.

Douglas MacArthur, Commander of the US-dominated UN force, seized the initiative and led a successful offensive, which quickly drove the communist forces out of South Korea.

MacArthur's success led to questions over US strategy: should the US settle for containment or aim to **rollback** communism? Truman authorised rollback and MacArthur crossed the 38th Parallel and headed towards the Chinese border.

Chinese intervention

Mao was determined to stop the UN force reaching the Chinese border. In October 1950 he mobilised a volunteer force to aid North Korea. Initially the Chinese pushed US forces back. However, Chinese successes were short-lived and the conflict reached a stalemate until the 1953 **armistice**.

The significance of the Korean War

The Korean War was significant for the development of the Cold War for the following reasons:

- It showed that the superpowers were prepared to commit military force to defend their interests.
- It showed that the superpowers wanted to avoid direct conflict and therefore were willing to use other nations and agencies to fight **'proxy wars'** on their behalf.
- It demonstrated the importance of domestic political pressure on US policy.

Key interpretation: US domestic politics

Some historians have linked the development of the Cold War to US domestic politics. Specifically, they point to the role played by Republicans and Democrats in the Truman administration and in Congress, and their attempts to win public support by exploiting Cold War fears. A key example is the China Lobby, who blamed Truman for 'losing China', forcing him to adopt a more aggressive stance against communism.

Below are a sample Part (b) exam-style question and the three sources referred to in the question. In one colour, draw links between the sources to show ways in which they agree about the importance of US domestic politics as a factor in the development of the Cold War. In another colour, draw links between the sources to show ways in which they disagree. Around the edge of the sources, write relevant own knowledge. Again, draw links to show the ways in which this agrees or disagrees with the sources.

Use Sources 1, 2 and 3 and your own knowledge.

How far do you agree with the view that US domestic politics was the main factor accounting for the development of the Cold War in the period 1945–1953?

SOURCE 1

(From Joseph M Siracusa in Into the Dark House, *published 1998)*

The onset of the Korean War, coupled with the 'loss' of China, played a major role in accelerating the US policy of containment. As Randall B. Woods put it, 'Had it not been for the fall of China and the Korean War, the Cold War as a fifty-year phenomenon involving the expenditure of billions of dollars and the destruction of millions of lives might never have happened.' The North Korean attack against South Korea on 25 June 1950 provided the Truman Administration with all the proof it needed that Stalin was on the move; the involvement of China in late November silenced critics of NSC-68 and ushered in a new, more dangerous world.

SOURCE 2

(From Warren I Cohen in America in the Age of Soviet Power 1945–1991, *published 1995)*

Stalin and his advisors, little understanding the United States, misjudged the American response [to the invasion of South Korea]. Arming the North Koreans and agreeing to their invasion of South Korea proved to be Stalin's most disastrous Cold War gamble. It postponed a thaw in relations with the United States for twenty years. It intensified a confrontation that continued for forty years at enormous cost to the major antagonists. The war shifted the balance of forces within the United States, allowing them to divert the attention and energies of the American people from needed reform to the hunt for Communists at home and abroad. It allowed the creation of a military-industrial complex that consumed the productive power of the American economy and fuelled conflict all over the world. The Korean War altered the nature of the Soviet-American confrontation, changing it from a systematic political competition into an ideologically driven, militarized contest that threatened the very survival of the globe.

SOURCE 3

(From Geoffrey Roberts in Stalin's Wars: From World War to Cold War, 1939–1953, *published 2007)*

Soviet foreign policy between 1948 and 1953 was a kaleidoscope of seemingly contradictory elements. The collapse of the Grand Alliance in 1947 provoked widespread fear that the cold war would soon develop into a 'hot war'. Stalin's own public statements warned of western warmongers, especially Churchill. But he also talked down the war danger and insisted on the possibility of the peaceful coexistence of communism and capitalism. In 1949 the Soviet Union tested its first atomic bomb – an event that coincided with an intense Soviet-sponsored peace campaign demanding disarmament and the abolition of nuclear weapons. The invasion [of Korea in 1950] had Stalin's blessing and support but when the United States intervened on South Korea's behalf he quickly backed away from direct confrontation with the Americans. [These contradictions are explained by the fact that] Stalin saw the cold war struggle as necessary to protect Soviet security and communist gains after the Second World War but feared that escalation of the conflict would result in an even greater danger: the revival of German militarism and its combination with an America-led western bloc.

⏺ Recommended reading

Below is a list of suggested further reading on this topic.

- *The Cold War,* chapters 1–3, Robert J McMahon (2003)
- *The Cold War: An International History,* chapter 2, David S Painter (1999)
- *The Origins of the Cold War 1941–49,* Martin McCauley (2008)

Exam focus

On pages 21–23 is a sample answer to the Part (b) exam-style question on this page. Read the answer and the examiner comments around it.

Use Sources 1, 2 and 3 and your own knowledge.

How far do you agree with the view that ideological competition between the superpowers accounts for the development of the Cold War in the years 1945–1953?

Explain your answer, using Sources 1, 2 and 3 and your own knowledge of the issues related to this controversy. (40 marks)

SOURCE 1

(From Joseph M Siracusa in Into the Dark House, *published 1998)*

The onset of the Korean War, coupled with the 'loss' of China, played a major role in accelerating containment. As Randall B. Woods put it, 'Had it not been for the fall of China and the Korean War, the Cold war as a fifty-year phenomenon involving the expenditure of billions of dollars and the destruction of millions of lives might never have happened.' The North Korean attack against South Korea on 25 June 1950 provided the Truman Administration with all the proof it needed that Stalin and his ilk was on the move; the involvement of China in late November silenced critics of NSC-68 and ushered in a new, more dangerous world.

SOURCE 2

(From Vladislav Zubok and Constantine Pleshakov in 'Stalin's Road to Cold War', in The Origins of the Cold War, *published 1999)*

Just one year after Yalta, in his first postwar speech, on February 9, 1946, Stalin emphasized the importance of ensuring Soviet security unilaterally – through renewed mobilization of domestic resources, and rearmament. There was only a dying echo of the early hopes for peaceful coexistence. The shift in Stalin's attitude towards postwar cooperation in 1945–6 can be attributed in part to his deep and morbid obsessions and compulsions. These compulsions were of immense international significance, since the power to dictate Soviet foreign policy belonged to Stalin alone.

SOURCE 3

(From David C Engerman, 'Ideology and the origins of the Cold War 1917–1962' in The Cambridge History of the Cold War, *eds. Melvyn P Leffler and Odd Arne Westad, published 2010)*

Russia's Great October Socialist Revolution of 1917 triggered a confrontation between the Soviet Union and the US that would last much of the twentieth century. In addition to competition over markets or territories the Cold War was at its root a battle of ideas: American liberalism vs. Soviet Communism. American and Soviet ideologies were set in direct opposition to each other, ensuring disagreement between the two countries. Americans understood Soviet expansion as a direct blow against freedom, while Soviet observers saw American expansion as proof that the final crisis of capitalism was near. The defeat of Nazi Germany in 1945 cleared the stage for the expansion of American-Soviet ideological conflict into a global Cold War.

Clearly, as Source 3 argues, ideological competition played a role in the development of the Cold War in the years 1945—1953. However, it was not the main factor in the development of superpower relations. The personality of Stalin, discussed in Source 2, and the pressures on Truman, the focus of Source 1, also played a key role. However, fundamentally, the development of the Cold War is best explained by mistrust and misunderstanding between the superpowers.

Source 3 overstates the significance of ideological conflict between the superpowers. In essence it argues that the conflict was rooted in ideology, 'American liberalism vs. Soviet Communism' — ideological positions that were 'set in direct opposition to each other'. Certainly, the ideology of the US, with its emphasis on individual freedom and free trade, was at odds with Soviet communism, which explicitly aimed at the overthrow of capitalism and the introduction of a planned economy. Nonetheless, Source 3 is wrong to argue that ideological differences had the effect of 'ensuring disagreement between the two countries'. There were on-going disagreements between the two countries from 1917, such as US intervention in the Russian Civil War (1918—1920), which was designed to end communist rule, and the Red Scare of 1919 in which zealous anti-communists tried to expel left-wing radicals from the US. However, there were also periods of peace and collaboration between the two powers. The Grand Alliance saw the US and the Soviet Union put aside their ideological differences in order to defeat the Axis Powers. Indeed, the conferences at Tehran, Yalta and Potsdam showed that the leaders of the US and the Soviet Union could work together in spite of their ideological differences. Moreover, Source 2's reference to 'early hopes for peaceful coexistence' indicates that even after Potsdam there was the possibility of continued co-operation. In this sense Source 3's argument that the 'Revolution of 1917 triggered a confrontation between the Soviet Union and the US that would last much of the twentieth century' is simplistic as the confrontation was not continuous, and there was a period of close collaboration during the Second World War. Consequently, ideological differences do not account for the development of the Cold War in the years 1945—1953 because the experience of the war showed that these supposedly fundamental differences could be overcome.

Source 2 focuses on Stalin's role in the development of the Cold War. It argues that his 'deep and morbid obsessions and compulsions' led to a breakdown in superpower relations and the emergence of the Cold War. In this sense, Source 2 claims that Stalin's decision to adopt a policy of 'mobilization of domestic resources, and rearmament' in order to ensure 'Soviet security unilaterally' marked an end to a more hopeful period in superpower relations and the beginning of the Cold War. Again, this interpretation is too simplistic. Source 2 implies that Yalta was a high point of superpower

The introduction refers to the interpretations offered by all three of the sources and provides an immediate answer to the question. This shows focus on the sources, alongside independence of thought.

Each of the main paragraphs begins with reference to the interpretations offered by the sources. In this sense, the sources are used to shape the argument of the essay.

Here, the candidate links the sources to their own knowledge, constructing an integrated response to the question.

Here, the candidate challenges the interpretation offered by Source 3, showing independence.

co-operation. However, other historians have argued that it was a turning point as it effectively divided Europe into two opposing spheres of influence. Additionally, Stalin's 'morbid obsession' with the security of the Soviet Union was based on worrying trends in US diplomacy. As Source 3 acknowledges, the Cold War was, in part, a 'competition over markets or territories', and the US was increasing its links with Japan and fighting to protect its sphere of influence. Moreover, important figures in the US administration were already arguing for a policy of 'containment'. As the 1940s went on, Stalin believed there was mounting evidence of the West's desire to crush communism. Stalin's suspicions were aroused by plans to introduce a new currency in Trizonia. The decision to stop paying reparations from Trizonia to the Soviet Union persuaded Stalin that his relationship with the West had broken down. Consequently, he reacted with aggressive policies such as the Berlin Blockade. In this way, suggesting that Stalin's 'obsessions and compulsions' were the main factor behind the development of the Cold War in the years 1945—1953 is simplistic because it ignores the international context in which Stalin was acting.

Source 1's argument that 'The onset of the Korean War, coupled with the "loss" of China' were significant in the development of the Cold War is a more plausible interpretation than the emphasis on ideology in Source 3 or the stress on Stalin's personality put forward in Source 2. Indeed, Source 1 is right to argue that events in Asia were significant because they confirmed the worst fears of policy makers in the US government. Specifically, they seemed to prove that Kennan's view that Stalin was preparing for world domination was correct. Events in Asia were also significant as they led to increased domestic pressure from the 'China Lobby' to be more assertive in policy towards the Soviet Union. Therefore, Source 1 points to the issue of misunderstanding that led to the deterioration of relations from 1945 to 1953. Broadly, following the Second World War, both superpowers were attempting to safeguard their positions. This explains Stalin's unwillingness to allow a democratic government in Poland, as well as his refusal to allow currency reform in Germany. These were not attempts to spread the revolution or overthrow capitalism; they were intended to ensure the Soviet Union's security. However, senior figures in the US, such as Kennan, misunderstood Stalin's intentions, assuming that his actions were ideologically motivated. Indeed, in this context there is some truth in Source 3's claims that ideology was an important factor in the conflict. Indeed, as Source 1 implies, ideology helped senior figures in the governments of both superpowers to interpret the actions of their opponent. Source 1 shows that US politicians understood 1949 and 1950 as a period in which Stalin and communism more generally were on the offensive. In 1949 the Soviet Union tested its first atomic bomb, destroying the US's nuclear monopoly. The US government was wrong to

At the end of each paragraph, the candidate links back to the question, showing sustained focus.

This paragraph begins by discussing another possible interpretation of the causes of the Cold War. It is important that Part (b) essays consider a range of possible interpretations.

Here, the sources are used in combination, to form a fully integrated response.

The own knowledge used is detailed, showing a confident grasp of the topic.

assume that the invasion of South Korea was part of some grand communist plan. Neither Stalin nor Kim was acting primarily ideologically. Kim was after power; he wanted to control the whole of Korea. Stalin agreed to the war as he knew that he could rely on Chinese forces to do the bulk of the fighting, and because the Soviet Union's nuclear success meant that the US was extremely unlikely to use its atomic bombs against the Soviet Union. Similarly, Stalin's pessimism in Source 2 was brought about by a misunderstanding of the US's intentions. Stalin was convinced that the US government was acting as an imperialist power. This is the view that was later put forward in the Novikov telegram. In this way the period of the escalation of the Cold War that occurred from 1946 to the Korean War was not the result of ideological conflict because both superpowers were acting pragmatically, rather than ideologically, to protect their own interests. Nonetheless, ideology did play a role in the mutual misunderstanding as, on both sides, there was an assumption that the opponent was acting ideologically.

Ultimately, the Cold War developed through a series of superpower actions that provoked reactions from their opponent. Therefore, Source 3 is right that ideology played a role in the development of the Cold War. However, it over-emphasises its significance. In reality ideology was significant, particularly in the US, as policy makers interpreted Stalin's policies and actions as a realisation of his ideology. In this sense ideology did not lead directly to the development of US or Soviet policy as Source 3 claims. Rather, it played an indirect role affecting the reactions of the two superpowers. Personalities also played a role as Source 2 claims. But the context of mistrust was more significant. As Source 2 argues, within a year of the Yalta conference, trust had broken down, and therefore the leaders of the two superpowers viewed each other with increasing suspicion. This suspicion coupled with their ideological understanding of each other's policies lead to the development of the Cold War.

The conclusion explains the relative importance of the different factors discussed, and makes links to the sources. Therefore, the essay concludes with a reasoned judgement.

40/40

This essay presents a sustained analytical response from own knowledge, showing an explicit understanding of the issues raised by the question. It integrates own knowledge with material from the sources. The candidate uses the sources with confidence, presenting and criticising the interpretations that they offer, in order to develop an independent argument.

Reverse engineering

The best essays are based on careful plans. Read the essay and the examiner's comments and try to work out the general points of the plan used to write the essay. Once you have done this, note down the specific examples used to support each general point.

Section 2: The post-Stalin thaw and the bid for peaceful coexistence

The Eastern bloc after Stalin

Stalin's death on 5 March 1953 raised the possibility of a change within the communist bloc and a new relationship between the two superpowers.

Following Stalin's death the Soviet government was dominated by two men:

- Georgy Malenkov, the chairman of the Council of Ministers
- Nikita Khrushchev, the secretary of the Central Committee.

Unrest in East Germany

The summer of 1953 saw a series of major protests and strikes across Eastern Europe. There was unrest in Bulgaria, Czechoslovakia and particularly the Soviet zone of Germany. These presented challenges to the new leaders in the **Kremlin**.

In East Germany, there were serious protests against **communism**. Walter Ulbricht, leader of East Germany, had embarked on an austere **socialist programme**, leading to low living standards and high levels of inflation. His decision to increase compulsory **work quotas** by 10 per cent triggered large-scale strikes and protests.

The new Soviet leaders summoned Ulbricht to Moscow and advised him to modify his policies. Ulbricht refused. When further protests exploded in June 1953, the Soviet leadership decided they had to back Ulbricht's regime. Consequently, the **Soviet Union** sent military forces to crush the anti-communist risings. This was a propaganda disaster for the Soviet Union.

The foundation of the Warsaw Pact, 1955

In May 1955, the Soviet Union created the **Warsaw Pact**. The Pact was a military alliance between the Soviet Union and seven Eastern European **satellite states**. The alliance was formed in response to the decision of West Germany to join **NATO** in October 1954, as Soviet leaders saw the enlargement of NATO as a threat.

Malenkov's 'New Course'

Malenkov recognised the need for the Soviet Union to improve the living standards of Soviet citizens. Consequently, he proposed diverting resources from defence to the production of consumer goods. In order to reduce the Soviet defence budget, he launched the 'New Course', an attempt to reduce **Cold War** tension and achieve **peaceful coexistence** with the West.

Peaceful coexistence

Peaceful coexistence was a new theory developed in the Soviet Union during the mid-1950s. It suggested that conflict between **capitalism** and communism was not inevitable. Khrushchev set out his understanding of the doctrine in the Communist Party Congress of 1956. Essentially, he reversed Stalin's view that war between capitalism and communism was inevitable, arguing that capitalism and communism could exist side by side without military conflict. The belief in peaceful coexistence led Soviet leaders to seek negotiated solutions with Western leaders and justified reducing defence budgets.

Soviet foreign policy under Malenkov

The 'New Course' led to a change in Soviet policy:

- In 1953, the new Soviet leadership contributed to the peace process in Korea, leading to an end to the Korean War (see page 18).
- In 1954, the new leadership gave up Soviet military bases in Finland.
- Soviet leaders worked to improve relations with **Marshal Tito** who had been determined that Yugoslavia would not become a satellite state of the Soviet Union and had therefore clashed with Stalin.
- In 1955, Austria, which had been divided after the Second World War, was reunited as a result of the **Austrian Treaty**. Consequently, the Russian army withdrew from Austria, and Austria was recognised as a neutral country.
- The Soviet army was cut by around 20 per cent. This was not linked to any equivalent cuts by the Western powers and aroused opposition from the Soviet military leadership.

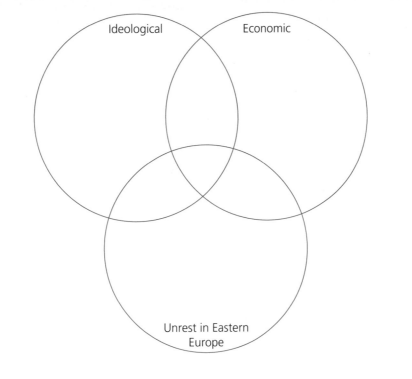

Complete the paragraph

Below are a sample exam-style question and a paragraph written in answer to this question. The paragraph contains a point and a concluding explanatory link back to the question, but lacks examples. Complete the paragraph, adding examples in the space provided.

Why did the Soviet leadership embrace 'peaceful coexistence' in the years following Stalin's death?

One reason why the Soviet leadership embraced 'peaceful coexistence' in the years following Stalin's death was linked to economic problems within the Soviet Union. For example,

_____

_____

_____

_____

In this way, economic problems within the Soviet Union led Soviet leaders to embrace 'peaceful coexistence' because they hoped that a better relationship with the US would allow them to reduce defence spending and thus improve Soviet living standards.

Complete the Venn diagram

Use the information on the opposite page to add detail to the Venn diagram below. In each area of the diagram, list reasons why the Soviet Union adopted peaceful coexistence. These reasons relate to ideology, the economy and unrest in Eastern Europe. In the intersecting areas of the diagram, show how these reasons overlapped.

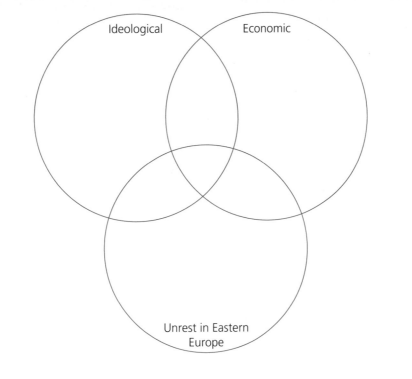

Ideological

Economic

Unrest in Eastern Europe

Eisenhower's 'New Look'

Eisenhower as president

Dwight D Eisenhower replaced Truman as president of the US in January 1953. Eisenhower had been Supreme Commander of the Allied forces in western Europe from 1943 and later the first commander of NATO. He came into office promising to stand up to communism.

Eisenhower's foreign policy

Eisenhower was determined to introduce a 'New Look' foreign policy. Indeed, he quickly initiated Operation Solarium, a full review of US policy options. He appointed an experienced foreign policy team led by Secretary of State John Foster Dulles. Operation Solarium established the following basic principles to guide US foreign policy:

- National security was to include the defence of democratic and capitalist values as well as geographical territory.
- There was great concern about the size of the defence budget inherited from Truman. Eisenhower felt it was vital to achieve the appropriate balance between defence needs and other spending priorities. Therefore, he decided to cut **conventional forces** and concentrate on the **nuclear arsenal**.

Eisenhower and nuclear weapons

Eisenhower was very clear about the significance of nuclear weapons. He had no illusions about the consequences of nuclear conflict and believed that the leaders in the Kremlin would not seek nuclear confrontation. Eisenhower had no time for the concept of **limited strikes**. He believed that the threat of **massive retaliation** would deter a Soviet offensive. He stated, 'We must only plan for total war because it is the only way to preclude any war'.

Fighting communism in the Third World

Eisenhower believed that nuclear weapons would deter war between the **First World** and the **Second World**. Nonetheless, he had a different approach to stopping communism in the **Third World**. He advocated the following:

- **Covert actions** would be planned and carried out by the **CIA**. During Eisenhower's presidency, the CIA was expanded from seven stations across the globe to 47. Between 1953 and 1958, the CIA intervened against perceived socialist threats in Iran and Guatemala. There was also a failed attempt to remove the **Sukarno regime** in Indonesia.
- A new network of alliances would be developed to safeguard the US's allies such as **SEATO** and **CENTO**.

Problems facing Eisenhower

As a result of his determination to cut spending, he expected that his allies would develop their own ground forces while the US supplied the **nuclear umbrella**. This did not always happen in practice, notably in Western Europe where other countries were also trying to cut their defence spending.

The US often confused Third World **nationalism** with communism. Consequently, the US missed opportunities to work with **nationalist** groups, leaving scope for the Soviets to move in. This was particularly evident in Asia and the Middle East.

In 1957, the Soviet Union won an important propaganda victory. They successfully tested an **Intercontinental Ballistic Missile (ICBM)** and launched **Sputnik** 1, the world's first artificial satellite. Consequently, fears began to grow that there was a **missile gap** and that the US was vulnerable. The political opponents of Eisenhower stoked up these fears and created an impression that the president had been negligent on his watch. In fact, **U2** surveillance flights showed clearly that there was no Soviet supremacy.

Simple essay style

Below is a sample exam-style question. Use your own knowledge and the information on the opposite page to produce a plan for this question. Choose four general points, and provide three pieces of specific information to support each general point. Once you have planned your essay, write the introduction and conclusion for the essay. The introduction should list the points to be discussed in the essay. The conclusion should summarise the key points and justify which point was the most important.

How far did Eisenhower's 'New Look' jeopardise 'peaceful coexistence' between the superpowers in the period 1953–1960?

Develop the detail (a)

Below is a sample exam-style question and a paragraph written in answer to this question. The paragraph contains a limited amount of detail. Annotate the paragraph to add additional detail to the answer.

Why did Eisenhower adopt the 'New Look' in 1953?

Eisenhower adopted the 'New Look' in 1953 in part due to concerns about nuclear war. The 'New Look' changed Truman's policy of limited strikes to a policy of massive retaliation. The limited strikes policy suggested that the US could launch weapons against specific targets. Massive retaliation, by contrast, suggested a policy of complete annihilation in response to a nuclear attack. In this way, one of the reasons why Eisenhower adopted the 'New Look' in 1953 was his concern to prevent nuclear war. Specifically, he adopted the policy of massive retaliation in an attempt to deter Soviet nuclear aggression.

Soviet policy under Khrushchev

Khrushchev emerged as Soviet leader in 1955. Malenkov was removed from the Soviet leadership after the failure of his policies in East Germany.

Khrushchev's personality

Khrushchev's personality played a big part in the development of the Cold War. His temperament was unpredictable. Indeed, he was known for his sudden explosions of anger. He did not always consult colleagues or think through his policies. He also had a tendency to make wild claims about the scale of the Soviet Union's nuclear arsenal. His erratic nature and crude manner of expression led to an attempt to remove him from the leadership in 1957.

President Eisenhower argued that Khrushchev's tough talk should not be taken too seriously. He argued that his violent words were a substitute for real action. He recognised that Khrushchev was under pressure from the Soviet government to stand up to the US.

Khrushchev's policies

Domestic aims

Khrushchev agreed with Malenkov that the Soviet Union's primary aim must be to revitalise the economy. This, along with his belief in peaceful coexistence, had massive implications for the conduct of foreign policy, including cuts in the defence budget. This created problems with some Kremlin **hardliners**, and also with leaders of the defence production industries.

Cold War diplomacy

Khrushchev's approach to the Cold War was inconsistent. Sometimes he used menacing phrases, threatening to 'bury' the West. On other occasions he was a passionate advocate of peaceful coexistence. It seems that his personal feelings often played a big part in his approach to the Cold War and undermined Soviet diplomacy.

The Third World

Given the cuts in military forces, Khrushchev needed to look for other ways for the Soviet Union to assert itself in foreign policy. The Third World offered opportunities:

- Khrushchev tried to create allies among the newly independent states in Asia and Africa.
- He recognised that the Middle East, with its vast oil reserves, was economically important for the Western powers. Therefore, he established links with Egypt's President Nasser, helping to fund the Aswan Dam project, in order to challenge Western dominance in the area.
- He built a relationship with Cuban revolutionary **Fidel Castro** after the Cuban Revolution of 1959.

The Secret Speech, 1956

On 25 February 1956 Khrushchev made a speech that began the process of **de-Stalinisation**. The speech criticised Stalin for establishing a '**cult of personality**', stating that Stalin had abused his position and perverted true communism. The speech had significant implications for the Cold War as it provided a spur for reformers in areas of Central and Eastern Europe.

As was often the case, Khrushchev had not thought through the implications of his points before he spoke. Western intelligence obtained a recording of the 'Secret Speech' and **Radio Free Europe** broadcast it across Eastern Europe and the Soviet Union. The speech breathed new life into the reformist groups across Eastern Europe, who hoped Khrushchev's words signalled a more liberal approach to the region. However, Khrushchev had no intention of losing control of Eastern Europe.

Eliminate irrelevance

Below are a sample exam-style question and a paragraph written in answer to this question. Read the paragraph and identify parts of the paragraph that are not directly relevant to the question. Draw a line through the information that is irrelevant and justify your deletions in the margin.

To what extent was Khrushchev committed to 'peaceful coexistence' with the US in the period 1956–1961?

Prior to 1956, Malenkov had pursued a policy of 'peaceful coexistence', signing the Austrian Treaty in 1955 and opening diplomatic channels in order to end the Korean War. Khrushchev's personality meant that he was only partially committed to 'peaceful coexistence' in the period 1956–1961. For example, he was temperamental and unpredictable. He was prone to sudden explosions of anger. He was erratic and rarely consulted colleagues on policy announcements. He was famous for his crudeness and had a tendency to make wild claims about the Soviet Union's nuclear arsenal. Khrushchev's personality undermined 'peaceful coexistence' because he was often aggressive in his dealings with the US. The president of the US at this time was Eisenhower. For example, the launch of Sputnik 1 in 1957 was an extremely provocative act which destabilised superpower relations. Khrushchev was not the only erratic personality involved in the Cold War. Mao Zedong also initiated rash policies such as the Great Leap Forward. In this way, Khrushchev's erratic personality meant that he was only partially committed to 'peaceful coexistence' because his temperamental behaviour tended to heighten tension between the Soviet Union and the US.

Introducing an argument

Below are a sample exam-style question, a list of key points to be made in the essay, and a simple introduction and conclusion for the essay. Read the question, the plan, and the introduction and conclusion. Rewrite the introduction and the conclusion in order to develop an argument.

How far was Khrushchev's personality the key reason for tensions between the Soviet Union and the US in the period 1956–1961?

Key points:

- Khrushchev's personality
- Ideological differences
- Superpower competition
- The 'New Look'

Introduction

There were four key reasons for tensions between the Soviet Union and the US in the period 1956–1961. These were Khrushchev's personality, ideological differences, superpower competition and the 'New Look'.

Conclusion

There were four key reasons for tensions between the Soviet Union and the US in the period 1956–1961. All of these reasons were of equal importance.

Poland and reform in Eastern Europe

Countries across Eastern Europe responded to the 'Secret Speech' by pushing for reform.

Unrest in Poland, 1956

Following the 'Secret Speech' the people of Poland began to challenge communist rule. The first serious uprising took place at Poznan, a mining community. The protest focused on:

- food shortages
- lack of consumer goods
- poor housing.

Khrushchev, alarmed at the situation, and under pressure himself from hardliners, led a delegation to Warsaw to reassert control. It had to deal with **Władysław Gomułka**, Poland's communist leader, and a very shrewd politician.

Gomułka made it clear to the Soviet delegation that the people of Poland were demanding reform. However, he emphasised that the reforms would not affect Poland's relationship with the Soviet Union. Specifically, he had no intention of:

- abandoning communism
- leaving the Warsaw Pact.

Radio Free Europe broadcast what had been achieved in Poland. Consequently, Gomułka became a hero to the student community in Budapest, which began to demand reform in Hungary.

Events in Hungary, 1956

Since the end of the Second World War, Hungary had been ruled by a hardline Stalinist, Rakosi. The new, more moderate Kremlin leadership was eager to replace him with a Moscow nominee, Gero. However, students demanded a new leader as they believed that Gero was too close to Khrushchev.

Imre Nagy emerged as the leading reformer. His initial proposals for reform were moderate.

However, as the momentum of the student movement grew he began to advocate a radical break with communism, including:

- a multi-party election system
- freedom for the press.

The political temperature rose and widespread violence broke out. There was a series of outrages against Communist Party officials, with some being hung from lamp posts.

Soviet reaction

The Soviets could not tolerate this situation and mobilised forces to take action. It was clear that Nagy was advocating much more radical reforms than Gomułka and that the communists had lost control of the situation. Consequently, on 4 November Soviet forces began to crush the rebellion. Nagy now announced withdrawal from the Warsaw Pact and made a direct appeal to the **United Nations** for support against the Soviet invasion.

Significance in the Cold War

The Hungarian crisis, in which 2700 people died, illustrates the determination of the Soviets to retain their overall control of Eastern Europe. However, it also shows that the Western powers were unwilling to act to support democratic reform in the **Eastern bloc**. Western leaders condemned Soviet intervention, but took no action. Eisenhower was preoccupied with his re-election campaign and unwilling to risk nuclear conflict. Therefore, he made public statements of support for Nagy, but refused to send military forces.

In spite of the West's inaction, the Hungarian crisis persuaded Western leaders that Soviet policy had not changed, and therefore that Soviet leaders had no real interest in peaceful coexistence.

Spectrum of significance

Below are a sample exam-style question and a list of general points which could be used to answer the question. Use your own knowledge and the information on the opposite page to reach a judgement about the importance of these general points to the question posed. Write numbers on the spectrum below to indicate their relative importance. Having done this, write a brief justification of your placement, explaining why some of these factors are more important than others. The resulting diagram could form the basis of an essay plan.

How far do you agree that Khrushchev's policies in Eastern Europe were the main reason for tensions in superpower relations in the period 1953–1961?

1. Khrushchev's policies in Eastern Europe
2. Khrushchev's personality
3. Superpower competition in the Third World
4. The foundation of the Warsaw Pact, 1955
5. Eisenhower's 'New Look'

Very important ←——————————————————————————————→ Less important

Developing an argument

Below is a sample exam-style question, a list of key points to be made in the essay, and a paragraph from the essay. Read the question, the plan and the sample paragraph. Rewrite the paragraph in order to develop an argument. Your paragraph should explain why the factor discussed in the paragraph is either more or less significant than the factor mentioned in the question.

How far do you agree that superpower competition in the Third World was the main reason for tensions in superpower relations in the period 1953–1961?

Key points:

- Khrushchev's policies in Eastern Europe
- Khrushchev's personality
- Superpower competition in the Third World
- The foundation of the Warsaw Pact, 1955
- Eisenhower's 'New Look'

Sample paragraph

Khrushchev's policies in Eastern Europe was certainly one factor that led to tensions in superpower relations in the period 1953–1961. In 1956, a student uprising in Hungary led to the emergence of Imre Nagy as Hungarian leader. Nagy soon adopted a radical reform agenda which had the potential to end communist rule in Hungary. Specifically, he argued in favour of freedom of the press, multiparty elections, and withdrawal from the Warsaw Pact. Khrushchev moved quickly to crush the rebellion and end Nagy's rule. On 4 November 1956, Soviet forces entered Hungarian territory to overthrow the government. In this way, the events caused tension between the superpowers as Eisenhower supported Nagy's government and condemned Khrushchev. Moreover, Khrushchev's reaction persuaded Western leaders that he was pursuing traditional Soviet policies and that his rhetoric of 'peaceful coexistence' was meaningless.

Summits from Geneva to Vienna

The Geneva Summit, 1955

The Geneva Summit of July 1955 was the first meeting of US and Soviet leaders since the Potsdam Conference of July 1945. The meeting was an attempt to resolve the status of Germany and begin negotiations about arms control.

Khrushchev took the initiative, reasserting Stalin's plan to create a united and neutral Germany. The US refused to accept this. West Germany had recently joined NATO and the US regarded it as central to the defence of Western Europe. In return, Khrushchev proposed disbanding NATO and the recently created Warsaw Pact. However, Eisenhower believed that NATO was essential to Western security.

Eisenhower countered by suggesting arms limitation treaties backed by an **'open skies' policy**. His proposal involved agreed limits on **superpower** military power. The superpowers would also authorise surveillance flights over each other's territory to check that the limits were being adhered to. Khrushchev rejected this proposal as he did not want the West to 'spy' on Soviet territory.

Although no agreement was reached, there was an acceptance of the **status quo** and an understanding that neither side wanted war. The two leaders agreed to meet again in Paris in 1960.

U2 incident

Fifteen days before the Paris Summit, Khrushchev announced that a US U2 spy plane had been shot down over Siberia. Assuming that the plane had been destroyed, Eisenhower released a cover story, claiming that the plane was a weather plane rather than a spy plane. However, Soviet forces had captured the plane and the pilot and were therefore able to prove that Eisenhower had lied to the public. Khrushchev won an important propaganda victory.

The Paris Summit, 1960

At the beginning of the summit, Khrushchev demanded an apology for the spying. Eisenhower stated that no such further missions would take place, but refused to apologise. Consequently, Khrushchev walked out of the summit. In his *Memoirs* Khrushchev singled out the U2 incident as the point at which Kremlin hardliners lost faith in 'peaceful coexistence'.

The Vienna Summit, 1961

The summit took place early in the presidency of **John F Kennedy**. Kennedy was determined to assert US strength due to the failure of his Cuban policy during the **Bay of Pigs** incident.

The Soviet position

Khrushchev regarded Berlin as the top priority. He was under pressure from Ulbricht, the leader of East Germany, to stop the exodus of East German citizens to West Germany via West Berlin. Indeed, since 1945, 2.7 million people had left East Germany. He was also keen to assert his authority at the summit by exploiting Kennedy's inexperience.

The US position

Disarmament was the US priority. At the Geneva Summit, Khrushchev had rejected Eisenhower's 'open skies' demands. Therefore, in order to help reach an agreement, Kennedy reduced the proposal from twenty annual inspections to ten.

The significance of the Vienna Summit

The talks failed to reach agreement on the status of West Berlin and on arms limitation. What is more, Khrushchev appeared to threaten Kennedy with military action if the US continued to support West Berlin. Kennedy used the opportunity to assert his hard-line position, stating, 'If all else fails in Berlin, we will use nuclear weapons.'

Below is a sample exam-style question which asks how far you agree with a specific statement. Below this is a series of general statements that are relevant to the question. Using your own knowledge and the information on the opposite page decide whether these statements support or challenge the statement in the question and tick the appropriate box.

'Khrushchev's diplomacy undermined "peaceful coexistence" in the period 1956–1961.' How far do you agree with this opinion?

	SUPPORT	CHALLENGE
Khrushchev proposed the reunification of Germany as a neutral state.		
Khrushchev was temperamental and erratic.		
Khrushchev tried to create Soviet allies in Asia and Africa.		
Khrushchev made an alliance with Fidel Castro following the Cuban Revolution.		
Khrushchev supported reform in Poland.		
Khrushchev ordered the invasion of Hungary.		
Khrushchev embarrassed the US during the U2 incident.		
Khrushchev rejected the 'open skies' policy.		
Khrushchev walked out of the Paris Summit.		
Khrushchev was unable to reach agreement with Kennedy at the Vienna Summit.		

Mind map

Use the information on the opposite page to add detail to the mind map below.

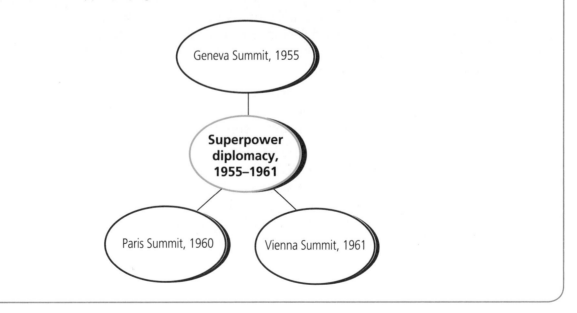

The Berlin Crisis, 1958–1962

Revised

The status of West Berlin

The status of West Berlin became contentious in the late 1950s due to West Germany's '**economic miracle**'. This led to two problems for Khrushchev.

- The growing self-assurance of the West German government manifested itself in military as well as economic developments. West Germany was building up its conventional forces and Franz Joseph Strauss, the Foreign Affairs Minister, was arguing for access to nuclear weapons. This provoked genuine alarm in the Soviet Union where there was still deep-seated apprehension of an economically strong and militarised Germany at the centre of Europe.

- An increasing number of East Germans were escaping to West Germany via West Berlin in order to benefit from West Germany's prosperity. Ulbricht, the East German leader, put pressure on Khrushchev to resolve this problem.

Khrushchev's policies

Khrushchev decided to address the Berlin situation. He needed to reassert his own position after the crises in Poland and Hungary, which many of the Kremlin hierarchy blamed on his 'Secret Speech' of 1956 (see page 28).

On 10 November 1958, Khrushchev made a speech referring to West Berlin as a 'malignant tumour requiring urgent surgery'. He delivered an ultimatum with a six-month deadline demanding that the Western powers demilitarise West Berlin. If they did not comply, Stalin would hand control of access rights to West Berlin to the East German regime.

The US response

Eisenhower made it clear that he would not give in to the demand. He emphasised to the Soviets that any provocative action would have drastic consequences.

The resolution of the Crisis

Khrushchev was unable to force the US to demilitarise West Berlin. Equally, he was not willing to start a war. Therefore, he backed Ulbricht's demand for a physical barrier dividing Berlin, designed to stop East Germans escaping to the West. In August 1961, construction began on the **Berlin Wall**.

The Berlin Wall became a symbol of division, and to some extent the most dramatic image of the Cold War. President Kennedy grasped that it was essentially a defensive measure. Khrushchev had stepped back from direct confrontation.

Kennedy was determined to show his solidarity with the citizens of West Berlin. On 26 June 1963, he visited West Berlin and made a speech to a crowd of over 300,000 Berliners. He was more confident after the resolution of the Cuban Missile Crisis (see page 42) the previous year and saw in the Wall a symbol of the stark differences between East and West: 'Freedom has many difficulties and Democracy is not perfect but we have never had to put up a wall to keep our people in.' He stated that the Wall represented a propaganda disaster for the East and made it clear that the US would stand by West Berlin.

Below are a sample exam-style question and a timeline. Read the question, study the timeline and, using three coloured pens, put a Red, Amber or Green star next to the events to show:

Red: Events and policies that have no relevance to the question
Amber: Events and policies that have some significance to the question
Green: Events and policies that are directly relevant to the question

1) How accurate is it to say that the superpowers achieved a state of 'peaceful coexistence' in the period 1953–1961?

Now repeat the activity with the following questions:

2) 'The Soviet leadership embraced the policy of "peaceful coexistence" primarily for economic reasons.' How far do you agree with this view?

3) How far did conflict over the status of Germany undermine 'peaceful coexistence' in the period 1955–1961?

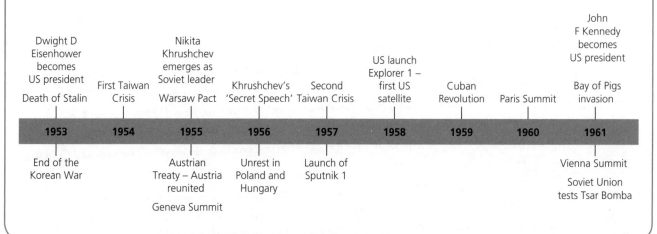

Below is a list of suggested further reading on this topic.

- *The Cold War,* chapter 4, Robert J McMahon (2003)
- *The Cold War,* chapter 3, Bradley Lightbody (1999)
- *The Soviet Union in World Politics, 1945–1991*, chapter 3, Geoffrey Roberts (1998)

Exam focus

Below is a sample A grade Part (a) essay. Read it and the examiner comments around it.

'The Soviet Union was never fully committed to "peaceful coexistence" in the years 1953–1961.' How far do you agree with this view? (30 marks)

The essay begins with an argument based on a clear definition of 'peaceful coexistence'. It links this to a sophisticated argument that is pursued for the rest of the essay.

The Soviet Union was committed to 'peaceful coexistence' in the years 1953–1961. This was first evident during the period of Malenkov's 'New Course' as well as becoming the official policy of the Soviet government under Khrushchev in 1956. However, it is also true that the period 1953 to 1961 witnessed continual tension between the US and the Soviet Union as both sides continued to re-arm and remained ready for war. However, according to Khrushchev's definition, 'peaceful coexistence' was achieved. Significantly, while Khrushchev and Malenkov were committed to 'peaceful coexistence' they were also committed to demonstrating the superiority of the Soviet system and safeguarding Soviet interests. Therefore, both were willing to pursue peaceful competition — even if it heightened Cold War tensions, and neither was willing to sacrifice Soviet interests in the pursuit of peace. Khrushchev set out his understanding of 'peaceful coexistence' at the 1956 Party Congress. In essence, he rejected Stalin's view that military conflict between capitalism and communism was inevitable. In this sense, his definition did not necessitate an end to the Cold War or an end to superpower competition; all it meant was that military conflict should be avoided. Therefore, in this very limited way 'peaceful coexistence' was achieved, even though superpower competition continued in other areas, and in some ways this heightened Cold War tensions.

The next two paragraphs distinguish between the period of collective leadership and the period after Khrushchev's emergence as leader. Importantly, this allows the candidate to distinguish between two different periods of Soviet policy, and draw attention to the fact that 'peaceful coexistence' evolved from one period to the next.

The period 1953 to 1955 saw a concerted attempt, on the part of the new Soviet leadership, to achieve 'peaceful coexistence'. This phase of 'peaceful coexistence' entailed a greater emphasis on improving diplomatic relations than the later period following Khrushchev's 1956 speech. Following Stalin's death a new collective leadership emerged under Malenkov and Khrushchev. Unlike Stalin, they wanted to improve Soviet living standards, and therefore they wanted to change economic priorities from military spending to consumer goods. Therefore, they attempted to improve diplomatic relations hoping that a more stable relationship would decrease military tensions and allow a reduction in military spending. Malenkov's 'New Course' attempted to ease superpower tensions and led to diplomatic efforts in 1953 to end the Korean War. Additionally, in 1954 the 'New Course' resulted in the Soviet Union giving up its bases in Finland. In 1955 the Soviet leadership initiated negotiations over the status of Austria, leading to the Austrian Treaty, which reunited Austria as a neutral country. Finally, the Soviet army was cut by 20 per cent. However, even during the 'New Course' the Soviet leadership continued to compete with the US. For example, in May 1955 the Soviet Union initiated the creation of the Warsaw Pact, a military alliance that united Eastern Europe against NATO. This led to greater superpower tension. Eisenhower, too, made strategic alliances such as SEATO and CENTO. In this way, Malenkov's 'New Course' was an important step towards achieving 'peaceful coexistence' because it led to the end of the Korean War and ended conflict over Austria. However, as the creation of the Warsaw Pact demonstrates, it was never designed to completely end superpower competition.

Khrushchev was also committed to 'peaceful coexistence'. However, Khrushchev was more willing to emphasise Soviet strength than Malenkov. As a result, superpower relations under Khrushchev were more competitive and therefore more tense. Initially, Khrushchev attempted to ease superpower tensions by negotiating the reunification of Germany as a neutral country. However, fearing a shift in the balance of power in Europe, the US rejected the deal. The failure of this initiative and Eisenhower's 'New Look' policy led Khrushchev to pursue a more competitive policy. Eisenhower's 'New Look' abandoned the strategy of limited nuclear strikes, a policy that assumed that small numbers of nuclear weapons could be used to eliminate individual targets. Instead, Eisenhower embraced the policy of 'massive retaliation,' which aimed at total annihilation. Eisenhower justified this policy by arguing that planning for total war was 'the only way to preclude any war.' Khrushchev responded with a display of Soviet technological superiority. Therefore, he launched Sputnik 1, the world's first artificial satellite, proving the superiority of Soviet missile technology. This led to greater tension in the relationship as the US public were horrified by the achievement and Eisenhower's political opponents put pressure on the President to take a tougher stance on the Soviet Union. Clearly, in the period 1956–1957 there was an increase in superpower tension, but nonetheless, Khrushchev continued to be committed to peaceful coexistence as he avoided military confrontation and only pursued peaceful forms of competition.

Finally, Khrushchev conducted his diplomacy with the US in the spirit of 'peaceful coexistence'. Certainly, he was prepared to use the U2 incident to embarrass Eisenhower at the 1960 Paris Summit, and he deliberately attempted to use Kennedy's inexperience to his advantage at the Vienna Summit of 1961. Nonetheless, this was wholly compatible with Khrushchev's understanding of peaceful coexistence, which allowed scope for the peaceful demonstration of Soviet superiority. Indeed, Khrushchev's rejection of measures that would have decreased tension was consistent with the policy as he primarily rejected initiatives that would have exposed Soviet weakness. For example, he rejected Eisenhower and Kennedy's 'open skies' proposals, as surveillance flights would have exposed the fact that the Soviet Union was behind in the nuclear arms race. Equally, Khrushchev's refusal to back down over the Berlin Crisis was an attempt to safeguard Soviet interests. Therefore, although Khrushchev took a hard-line diplomatic position against Eisenhower and Kennedy, it was consistent with his understanding of 'peaceful coexistence' because safeguarding Soviet interests was essential to his understanding of the policy.

In conclusion, it is clear that the Soviet Union was fully committed to 'peaceful coexistence' in the years 1953–1961. Indeed, peaceful coexistence was never intended to end the Cold War, and therefore continued superpower tension does not show a lack of commitment on the part of either Malenkov or Khrushchev. Moreover, for both leaders 'peaceful coexistence' was compatible with peaceful competition, even if this heightened tension between the superpowers, and the policy was never intended to sacrifice Soviet advantage.

Here, the candidate notes the impact of US policy on the development of the Soviet approach to 'peaceful coexistence'.

This paragraph presents sustained analysis by linking its discussion of peaceful coexistence back to the definition given in the introduction.

The conclusion reiterates the argument that has run throughout the essay. However, it does not draw on the full range of material used in the essay and therefore is comparatively weak.

27/30

This essay is awarded a mark in Level 5 due to the fact that it advances a sustained analytical argument. Additionally, a good range and depth of supporting information guarantees it a secure mark in Level 5. However, the relatively weak conclusion means that the essay does not achieve maximum marks. The conclusion is weak because it does not do justice to the argument of the whole essay, focusing instead on a brief recap of the main argument. For a higher mark, the candidate would need to draw closer links between the argument and the material in the essay.

Key terms

One of the reasons why this essay is so successful is that it contains in the introduction a clear definition of the term in the question. Another example of an essay question involving a key term is below. Draw up a plan for your answer to this question. Include a definition of the key term in your introduction and refer back to this definition in subsequent paragraphs.

How accurate is it to say that Eisenhower's 'New Look' foreign policy increased tensions between the superpowers in the period 1953–1960?

The development of nuclear warheads

Nuclear weapons were central to the **Cold War**, and in a sense, the **arms race** became a substitute for real military conflict between the **superpowers**.

The atomic bomb

The US **Manhattan Project**, initiated during the Second World War, led to the creation of the first **atomic bombs**, which were used to bomb the Japanese cities of Hiroshima and Nagasaki in 1945. Stalin was determined to follow suit and make the **Soviet Union** a nuclear power. In August 1949, the Soviet Union successfully tested an atomic device, ending the US **nuclear monopoly**.

The hydrogen bomb

Following the Soviet test, Truman commissioned the development of the **hydrogen bomb** (H-bomb). This second generation of nuclear weapons were based on **nuclear fission** and therefore known as **thermo-nuclear devices**. The US's **Mike Tests** of November 1952 resulted in a **megaton** explosion, 1000 times that of the explosion at Hiroshima, producing a fireball 5.23 kilometres wide and a mushroom cloud that rose to 41,000 metres in three minutes.

Again, the Soviet Union was determined to keep up with US technology and it produced its own H-bomb within a year. The Soviet testing took place in Kazakhstan on 12 August 1953. The Soviet Union exploded a 400-kiloton device known as Joe 4. The test of **Andrei Sakharov's Third Idea** in November 1955 demonstrated that the Soviet Union had developed a bomb as powerful as the US H-bombs.

The arms race, 1950–1960

Throughout the 1950s, both superpowers regarded the development of firepower as vital to their security.

The US

- In the period 1950 to 1960, the number of US **warheads** increased from 1000 to 18,000.
- The first **battlefield tactical nuclear weapons** were stationed in West Germany in 1953.

- President **Eisenhower** developed the strategy of **massive retaliation**. He believed that a huge **nuclear arsenal** capable of annihilating the Soviet Union would deter a nuclear attack.

The Soviet Union

In 1961, in an aggressive speech designed to put pressure on President **John F Kennedy**, Khrushchev announced the successful testing of a 50-megaton bomb. This device, often referred to as the **Tsar Bomba**, was in fact 58 megatons. However, it was not a practical military option. A **CIA** report confirmed the power of the weapon, but also emphasised that it could not be loaded onto any **Intercontinental Ballistic Missile (ICBM)**, and could only be used by aircraft in test conditions.

The impact of weapons development

- Nuclear weapons became central to the development of the military strategy of both superpowers.
- The arms race increased tensions between the superpowers as they competed to gain a decisive lead.
- Consequently, a **balance of terror** existed between the superpowers, deterring direct military conflict which could potentially escalate into nuclear war.
- With the exception of West Berlin, which was Western territory situated within Stalin's **sphere of influence**, the threat of war forced the superpowers to respect each other's sphere of influence.
- The vast cost of developing both the weapons and the delivery systems put huge strain on the economies of the superpowers.
- Neither the US nor the Soviet Union was able to develop delivery systems powerful enough to attack each other directly. Consequently, prior to 1960, nuclear tensions focused on Central Europe – the only area within range of both superpowers.

Use the information on the opposite page to add detail to the mind map below.

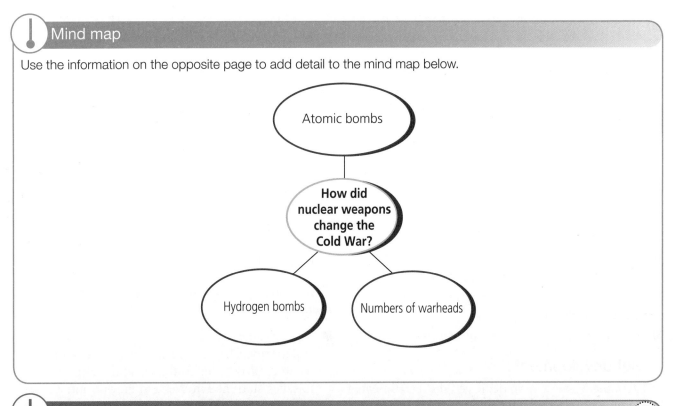

 | Eliminate irrelevance

Below are a sample exam-style question and a paragraph written in answer to this question. Read the paragraph and identify parts of the paragraph that are not directly relevant to the question. Draw a line through the information that is irrelevant and justify your deletions in the margin.

 'By 1960, the nuclear arms race had created a balance of terror between the superpowers.' How far do you agree with this view?

By 1960, there was a balance of terror between the superpowers in terms of hydrogen bombs. The US developed hydrogen bombs in 1952. The 1952 Mike Tests successfully exploded a hydrogen bomb 1000 times as powerful as the one exploded at Hiroshima. Within a year, the Soviet Union had tested its own hydrogen bomb in Kazakhstan. However, the Joe 4 explosion of 12 August 1953 was only 400 kilotons, compared to the Mike Tests, which created a 1-megaton explosion. In this sense, there was an imbalance of power until November 1955, when the Soviet Union tested Andrei Sakharov's Third Idea, creating an explosion as large as the Mike explosion. The balance of terror was a notable feature of the Cold War because the Soviet leadership, which was dominated by Malenkov and Khrushchev, was committed to 'peaceful coexistence'. Therefore, creating a balance of terror was contradictory to Malenkov's 'New Course', which led to the ending of war in Korea and the removal of Soviet military bases in Finland. In this way, by 1960, the development of hydrogen bombs had created a balance of terror as both sides had equal explosive capacity.

Delivery systems and the origins of the Cuban Missile Crisis

During the 1950s, both superpowers created ever more powerful warheads. However, neither side had a convincing delivery system capable of targeting the other superpower directly. The search for an effective delivery system was one of the causes of the Cuban Missile Crisis of 1962.

Delivery systems

During the 1950s and 1960s the superpowers developed four delivery systems:

- strategic bombers
- ICBMs fired from underground bases
- short-range nuclear missiles stationed outside the territory of the superpowers
- ballistic missiles fired from submarines.

Soviet developments

In 1956, the Soviet Union deployed the TU20 Bear, a long-range bomber which could reach US territory from Soviet air bases. However, the bombers were slow and could be intercepted by US fighter planes.

The problems inherent in **bomber technology** led to the development of ICBMs. The first successful Soviet ICBM test occurred in May 1957. Later in the year, the launch of **Sputnik** demonstrated to the world that Soviet missiles were powerful enough to reach space. This caused shock and panic in the US as it showed that the Soviet Union had the potential to target the US directly. However, ICBMs were expensive to produce and therefore Khrushchev attempted to find cheaper alternatives.

US developments

US ICBM technology lagged behind that of the Soviet Union in the mid-1950s and therefore the US focused on deploying **Intermediate Range Ballistic Missiles (IRBMs)**. IRBMs had a smaller range than ICBMs, but could target Soviet territory as they were stationed in Europe and the Middle East. However, by the early 1960s the US had developed ICBMs that were superior to the Soviet equivalents and therefore had a decisive lead in the arms race.

Key US developments included:

- the creation of the long-range bomber, the B52 Stratofortress, in 1955 – this was capable of reaching Soviet territory from US bases
- the launch of Explorer 1, the first US satellite in 1958
- the deployment of Polaris submarines, which could fire missiles from the ocean, in 1960
- the successful test of the Minuteman ICBM in 1961, which was capable of striking Soviet territory from the US.

The causes of the Cuban Missile Crisis

- Soviet leaders were aware of US nuclear superiority. The US could attack Soviet cities using ICBMs based in the US and shorter-range missiles stationed in Western Europe and Turkey. In contrast, the Soviet Union had only a limited number of ICBMs and no shorter-range missiles within range of the US. The Cuban Revolution of 1959, which led to the creation of a communist regime under **Fidel Castro**, gave Khrushchev an opportunity to achieve **nuclear parity**. Stationing nuclear missiles on Cuba, less than 160 kilometres away from the US, would allow the Soviet Union to target the US without having to use expensive long-range ICBMs. It would also double the capacity of the Soviet Union to hit targets in the US. Therefore, Khrushchev planned to send 40 tactical nuclear missiles and 50,000 Soviet soldiers to Cuba.

- Khrushchev was also determined to sustain Castro's communist regime. The US had attempted to overthrow Castro twice via a CIA-backed invasion of the **Bay of Pigs** and through **Operation Mongoose**. Khrushchev believed that sending nuclear weapons to Cuba would deter US interference.

- Finally, Khrushchev felt that a presence in Cuba could put pressure on the US to surrender West Berlin and withdraw its missiles from Turkey.

Simple essay style

Below is a sample exam-style question. Use your own knowledge and the information on the opposite page to produce a plan for this question. Choose four general points, and provide three pieces of specific information to support each general point. Once you have planned your essay, write the introduction and conclusion for the essay. The introduction should list the points to be discussed in the essay. The conclusion should summarise the key points and justify which point was the most important.

How far was the development of delivery systems the main reason for increasing instability in superpower relations in the period 1957–1963?

Support or challenge?

Below is a sample exam-style question which asks how far you agree with a specific statement. Below this is a series of general statements which are relevant to the question. Using your own knowledge and the information on the opposite page decide whether these statements support or challenge the statement in the question and tick the appropriate box.

'By 1961, the US was the clear winner of the arms race.' How far do you agree with this opinion?

	SUPPORT	CHALLENGE
The US stationed battlefield nuclear weapons in West Germany from 1953.		
In 1955, Sakharov's Third Idea equalled the explosive capacity of US H-bombs.		
In 1956, the Soviet Union developed a long-range bomber that equalled the US B52 Stratofortress.		
The US launched Explorer 1 in 1958.		
In 1960, the US deployed Polaris submarines.		
In 1961, the US successfully tested its Minuteman ICBM.		
In 1961, the Soviet Union tested the 58-megaton hydrogen bomb, Tsar Bomba.		

The Cuban Missile Crisis, 1962

The development of the Crisis

In August 1962, Soviet nuclear warheads began to arrive in Cuba. They were followed in September by missiles and bombers. US spy planes spotted Soviet activity in October.

Superpower confrontation

President Kennedy responded to the Soviet build-up with a TV address in which he referred to 'unmistakable evidence of nuclear strike capability' on Cuba. He made it clear that 'a full retaliatory response' would follow if the Soviets did not abandon their military presence.

Rather than ordering immediate military action, Kennedy decided to establish a naval blockade. Aware that Soviet ships were en route to Cuba, he stated that any ships crossing the line would have to submit to US inspection. Khrushchev was relieved that Kennedy did not announce immediate military action.

The first potential flashpoint occurred on 24 October. Soviet ships reached the US **quarantine line**. At this point, the Soviet ships changed course, prompting the US Secretary of State Dean Rusk to remark, 'We are eyeball to eyeball and I think the other fellow just blinked'.

Resolution

On Thursday 25 October, attention focused on the **UN Security Council** where clashes took place between US Ambassador Stevenson and Soviet Ambassador Zorin. Stevenson appealed to the 'courtroom of world opinion', producing photographic evidence of the developing Soviet sites. Kennedy felt that by involving the **United Nations**, international opinion would turn against the Soviet Union.

On Friday 26 October, the White House received a long and rambling telegram from Khrushchev. The message proposed a way out of the Crisis that would involve a US guarantee not to invade Cuba. Before the US could decide on a response a second message was broadcast on Moscow Radio in a very different tone. This condemned the 'American imperialists'. It was decided to ignore the second message and regard the first as an indication of a desire to resolve the Crisis peacefully.

Kennedy's diplomacy

Throughout the Crisis, Kennedy was trying to negotiate with the Soviet leadership through **back channel meetings** between **Robert Kennedy** and the new Soviet ambassador to Washington, Anatoly Dobrynin. The back channel talks led to a compromise. The US agreed to withdraw its missiles from sites in Turkey in return for Soviet military withdrawal from Cuba. The US also agreed to respect Cuban independence and the Soviets agreed that there would be no public statement about the withdrawal of US missiles from Turkey. Consequently, on Sunday 28 October, the Soviets announced their withdrawal from Cuba.

> ### Saving face
>
> During the Cuban Missile Crisis, both leaders were seeking to avoid war without losing face. Khrushchev's actions had not been designed to cause war. He had assumed that the US would only discover Soviet missiles on Cuba once they were operational. Equally, Kennedy's prime objective was to avoid war. His actions were designed to contain the situation without provoking a military response from Khrushchev.
>
> Kennedy knew that Khrushchev would only back down if he could do so with dignity. Consequently, Kennedy ordered that there should be 'no boasting, no gloating, not even a claim of victory' on the part of the US. In this sense, Kennedy was attempting to reduce Khrushchev's humiliation and minimise tension between the superpowers.

Develop the detail

Below is a sample exam-style question and a paragraph written in answer to this question. The paragraph contains a limited amount of detail. Annotate the paragraph to add additional detail to the answer.

Why did superpower relations reach crisis point over Cuba during 1962?

> One reason why superpower relations reached crisis point over Cuba during 1962 was that the Soviet Union stationed nuclear missiles on Cuba. US spy planes spotted Soviet missiles. Kennedy realised that this increased the Soviet Union's capacity to strike the US. Indeed, Khrushchev planned to send a total of 40 tactical nuclear missiles to Cuba. As Cuba was not far away from the US, these missiles endangered most major US cities. In this way, the stationing of Soviet nuclear missiles on Cuba was one reason why superpower relations reached crisis point in 1962 because Kennedy realised that they posed a massive threat to US security, cutting the US advantage in the arms race.

Introducing an argument

Below are a sample exam-style question, a list of key points to be made in the essay, and a simple introduction and conclusion for the essay. Read the question, the plan, and the introduction and conclusion. Rewrite the introduction and the conclusion in order to develop an argument.

Why did superpower relations reach crisis point over Cuba during 1962?

Key points:

- An arms race had developed between the superpowers.
- The Soviet Union had fallen behind in the arms race.
- The Soviet Union stationed nuclear missiles on Cuba.
- Kennedy established a naval blockade.
- There were poor lines of communication between the leaders of the superpowers.

Introduction

> There were five key reasons why superpower relations reached crisis point over Cuba during 1962. These were the fact that an arms race had developed between the superpowers, the Soviet Union had fallen behind in the arms race, the Soviet Union stationed nuclear missiles on Cuba, Kennedy established a naval blockade, and there were poor lines of communication between the leaders of the superpowers.

Conclusion

> There were five key reasons why superpower relations reached crisis point over Cuba during 1962. All of these reasons were of equal importance.

The consequences of the Crisis

The Cuban Missile Crisis had a series of consequences. Kennedy and Khrushchev were both concerned about how close the world had come to nuclear war, and sought measures to minimise the possibility of nuclear conflict.

The Nuclear Test Ban Treaty, 1963

The Nuclear Test Ban Treaty was designed as a first step towards controlling nuclear arsenals. The Treaty banned the testing of nuclear weapons as a first step towards arms control. The Treaty banned:

- tests in the atmosphere
- tests in space
- tests under water.

Underground testing was permitted on the condition that no radioactive debris fell outside the country carrying out the test.

Significantly, there was no reduction in armaments. Stockpiling of warheads and future production was allowed and it was made clear that none of the agreements should prevent states taking any action in defence of their own security. Nonetheless, both sides committed themselves to continued negotiations with a view to **nuclear disarmament**.

The hot line

Both sides agreed to the establishment of a hot line between the US president and the Soviet leader. This was intended to improve communication and create an effective means for resolving problems.

Change in Soviet military policy

The Crisis contributed to a change in Soviet military policy. Soviet leaders believed that Khrushchev's diplomacy had resulted in a humiliating climb-down. Specifically, they believed that Khrushchev's policies in Cuba had led to a confrontation that the Soviet Union could not win – US nuclear superiority meant that the Soviet Union had to accept US terms. Consequently, Leonid Brezhnev, the new Soviet leader, changed Soviet policy, stepping up the production of warheads and missiles with the aim of achieving nuclear parity with the US.

New stability

From 1958 to 1963, the two superpowers came close to war on two occasions: over Berlin (see page 34) and over Cuba. Gerard DeGroot, historian of the nuclear bomb, argues that these years of maximum nuclear danger were caused by the relative weakness of the Soviet nuclear arsenal. He argues that nuclear disparity caused instability as:

- US generals advised aggressive policies as they assumed that in the event of war the US would be victorious
- Khrushchev adopted aggressive policies in order to cover up the Soviet nuclear inferiority. In this sense, Khrushchev's strident policies were a bluff, designed to make Western leaders believe that the Soviet Union was in a stronger position than it really was.

Consequently, the achievement of nuclear parity in the mid-1960s removed the causes of instability. Additionally, nuclear parity led to the prospect of a war in which both superpowers were utterly annihilated. Therefore, military strategists embraced the doctrine of **mutually assured destruction (MAD)**. Thus, the achievement of nuclear parity ended the era of nuclear crisis. Indeed, in the period 1964 to 1979 there were no further nuclear crises.

Kennedy and Khrushchev

The Crisis also changed the fortunes of the two leaders. Kennedy was praised for securing a peaceful resolution of the Crisis without backing down. By contrast, leading figures in the Soviet government criticised Khrushchev for leading the Soviet Union into an unwinnable confrontation and therefore damaging its prestige and credibility. Indeed, Khrushchev's role in the Missile Crisis was a major cause of his removal from office in 1964.

RAG – Rate the timeline

Below are a sample exam-style question and a timeline. Read the question, study the timeline and, using three coloured pens, put a Red, Amber or Green star next to the events to show:

Red: Events and policies that have no relevance to the question

Amber: Events and policies that have some significance to the question

Green: Events and policies that are directly relevant to the question

1) 'The nuclear arms race fundamentally destabilised superpower relations in the period 1949–1963.' How far do you agree with this view?

Now repeat the activity with the following questions:

2) How far had the superpowers established a balance of nuclear terror by 1963?

3) How far was the development of delivery systems the most significant feature of the arms race in the period 1949–1963?

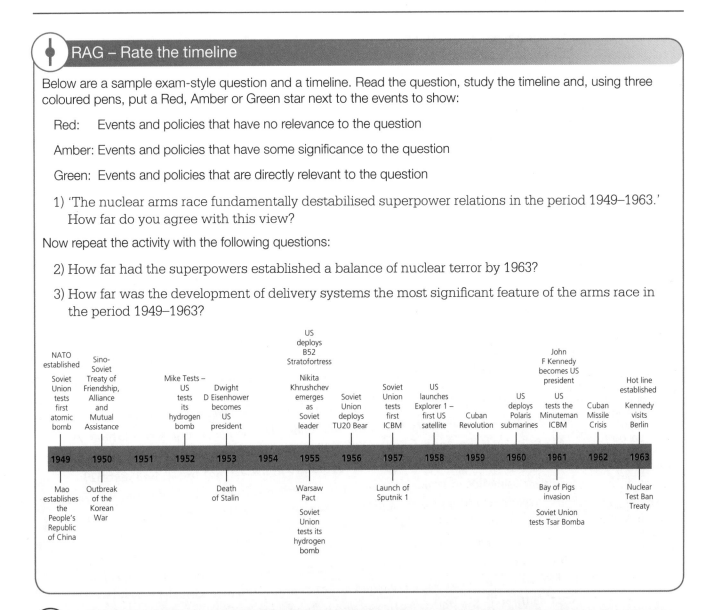

Recommended reading

Below is a list of suggested further reading on this topic.

- *The Cold War*, pages 90–97, Robert J McMahon (2003)
- *The Cold War*, pages 80–88, Mike Sewell (2002)
- *The Bomb: A Life*, chapters 11 and 12, Gerald DeGroot (2011)

Exam focus

Below is a sample A grade Part (a) essay. Read it and the examiner comments around it.

'The nuclear arms race fundamentally destabilised superpower relations in the period 1949–1963.' How far do you agree with this view? **(30 marks)**

The introduction focuses on the question immediately, and introduces the argument that will be sustained throughout the essay.

The nuclear arms race undoubtedly destabilised superpower relations in the period 1949–1963. The superpowers came close to nuclear war on four occasions during the period: the Berlin Crisis, the Korean War, the Taiwan Strait Crisis and the Cuban Missile Crisis. Indeed, the repeated crises that occurred during this time indicate that this was a period of considerable instability. However, the fact that the superpowers never engaged in a direct war indicates that the 'balance of terror' created through the nuclear arms race stabilised the relationship. In general, the arms race brought a measure of stability to superpower relations between 1949 and 1953 as it prevented war. However, the massive escalation of the arms race in the late 1950s and early 1960s, and the commanding lead established by the US, had a destabilising effect during the second half of this period.

This paragraph shows detailed knowledge of the period 1949–1953, and draws together knowledge of the arms race and the origins of the Cold War mentioned in Section 1 of this book.

Between 1949 and 1953 there was a rough balance of military power between the two superpowers and therefore the arms race tended to stabilise superpower relations. A key example is the Berlin Crisis of 1948–1949. The Soviet army was certainly powerful enough to take West Berlin by force. Yet Stalin was aware that the US had sent B29 bombers, capable of striking the Soviet Union with nuclear bombs, to Britain. As a result Stalin avoided actions that would lead to war as he did not want to provoke nuclear retaliation. The test of the Soviets' first atomic bomb in 1949 also helped to stabilise relations during the Korean War, by creating a nuclear balance of terror. Notably, the Korean War was not a direct conflict between the US and the Soviet Union. Fear of nuclear attack led the US to avoid direct conflict with a communist power by acting through the United Nations. Equally, the Soviet Union avoided direct conflict with the US by sponsoring first North Korean and then Chinese forces. In this sense, although the Korean War was an expression of the global conflict between capitalism and communism, the US and the Soviet Union were able to avoid war. In this way, the nuclear arms race brought a measure of stability to superpower relations in the period 1949–1953 because the threat of nuclear attack forced Stalin and Truman to limit their conflict, by avoiding direct conflict or policies that would lead to dramatic escalation.

Having considered the period 1949–1953, the candidate turns to the period 1953–1955. Again, the candidate draws on evidence from another section of the book – this time, Section 2.

The nuclear arms race also led the leaders of the Soviet Union to seek to establish better relations with the US in the period 1953–1955. The US Mike Tests of November 1952 demonstrated the power of a new kind of nuclear bomb. The hydrogen bomb resulted in an explosion 1000 times bigger than the atomic bomb that exploded at Hiroshima. The Soviet leaders knew that they had to catch up. They tested their first H-bomb, Joe 4, in Kazakhstan on 12 August 1953. At 400 kilotons it failed to match the US bomb. Andrei Sakharov's Third Idea, tested in November 1955, was the first Soviet bomb to deliver a megaton of explosive power. However, the Soviet success came at a massive cost to its economy. Indeed, as the Soviet economy was significantly smaller than the US economy, it was hit harder by the arms race in general. Therefore, the new Soviet leadership, headed by Malenkov and Khrushchev, sought 'peaceful coexistence' with the US in order to reduce tensions and scale back their massive military spending. The new policy led to an end of hostilities in Korea, and the reunification of Austria in 1955. Evidently, the nuclear arms race led to greater stability in superpower relations between 1953 and 1955 because the massive cost of developing hydrogen bombs forced the Soviet government to seek better relations with the US.

However, between 1956 and 1963 the nuclear arms race tended to destabilise the relationship between the superpowers. Eisenhower's 'New Look' approach to defence policy committed the US to shifting its military budget from conventional forces to nuclear weapons. Eisenhower was committed to a policy of 'Massive Retaliation', which meant that in the event of war he would authorise a nuclear strike so big that the Soviet Union would be annihilated. During this period, the number of US warheads increased to 18,000, far in excess of the Soviet stockpile. Additionally, Eisenhower also commissioned Polaris submarines which could attack the Soviet Union from the sea. By the late 1950s the US had a clear lead in the nuclear arms race. Khrushchev, aware of the weakness of his position, responded with some impressive demonstrations of Soviet power. These included the launch of Sputnik in 1957 and the detonation of the 58-megaton Tsar Bomba in 1961. Furthermore, the disparity of power led Khrushchev to station nuclear weapons on Cuba. Khrushchev believed that he could close the gap between the US and the Soviet Union by stationing relatively cheap Medium Range Ballistic Missiles on Cuba, within striking distance of the US, rather than producing large numbers of expensive Intercontinental Ballistic Missiles. The destabilising effect of the imbalance in the arms race was even more obvious during the ensuing Missile Crisis, as Khrushchev, aware of the weakness of his position, was unwilling to back down for fear of exposing the Soviet Union's nuclear limitations. In this way, the nuclear arms race tended to destabilise the relationship between the superpowers in the years 1956 to 1963 as Khrushchev's awareness of Soviet weaknesses pushed him to initiate threatening stunts and made him reluctant to back down during the Cuban Missile Crisis.

Overall, the nuclear arms race was not responsible for destabilising superpower relations in the period 1949–1963. Between 1949 and 1955 the nuclear arms race tended to limit conflicts, and even persuaded the new Soviet leaders to negotiate with the US. However, in the period 1956 to 1963 it led to a more dangerous relationship that reached its climax in the Cuban Missile Crisis. The key factor was not the nuclear arms race itself, but the imbalance of power. In the period where there was a military balance of terror the relationship was reasonably stable; it became dangerously unstable between 1956 and 1963 when the US lead in the arms race led Khrushchev to behave ever more aggressively in order to mask the Soviet Union's weakness.

This paragraph considers the impact of the arms race on the instability of the period 1956–1963. It sustains the argument developed in the introduction.

The conclusion pulls together the argument that was initiated in the introduction and developed throughout the essay. In this sense, the essay presents a consistent argument.

30/30

This is a Level 5 essay due to the fact that it has a clear argument that is sustained throughout the essay. It suggests that the arms race itself did not necessarily destabilise superpower relations. Rather, the imbalance of terror towards the end of the period was the key destabilising factor. In this sense, the argument is sophisticated as it acknowledges that the situation changed over time. The range and depth of supporting material ensure that this receives a mark at the very top of the level.

Reverse engineering

The best essays are based on careful plans. Read the essay and the examiner's comments and try to work out the general points of the plan used to write the essay. Once you have done this, note down the specific examples used to support each general point.

Section 4: Sino-Soviet relations, 1949–1976

Sino-Soviet relations, 1949–1956

In 1949 the balance of power in the Cold War shifted with the creation of a communist government in China. The US viewed the People's Republic of China (**PRC**) as a threat, a natural ally of the Soviet Union. However, Mao Zedong, the leader of China, was a **nationalist** as well as a communist. Therefore his relationship with the **Soviet Union** was more complex than the US anticipated.

Mao and Stalin

Mao respected Stalin as leader of the communist world. Nonetheless, Mao had been frustrated by Stalin's failure to support the communists during the **Chinese Civil War**. Equally, Stalin was suspicious of Mao. Stalin feared that Mao might adopt policies that damaged the interests of the Soviet Union. In addition, the Soviet Union and China had a competing desire to be the leading power in Asia, and therefore the relationship was difficult.

Treaty of Friendship, Alliance and Mutual Assistance

Stalin and Mao were able to work together for three reasons:

■ Mao respected Stalin.

■ Other world powers, such as Britain and the US, refused to work with communist countries, therefore Mao had no alternative allies.

■ As communists, Mao and Stalin had common enemies.

Consequently, in 1950 Mao and Stalin signed the Treaty of Friendship, Alliance and Mutual Assistance. Although China gained a powerful ally, Mao felt that the Treaty favoured the Soviet Union.

The terms of the Treaty

- China accepted Soviet leadership of the communist world.
- China and the Soviet Union formed a military pact against invasion from capitalist nations.
- China was to be given economic and technical aid, and help with developing an air force. However, under the terms of the agreement, this aid was to be repaid at a high rate of interest.
- China's sovereignty in **Manchuria** was restored.
- Mongolia remained in the Soviet **sphere of influence**.

The Korean War

The Korean War (see page 18) was the first test of the new alliance. Stalin wanted to avoid a direct military confrontation between the two **superpowers**. At the same time he did not want communist North Korea to be defeated. Mao's willingness to send a volunteer force of 270,000 to defend North Korea allowed Stalin to achieve both of his objectives.

The conflict was highly significant for Sino-Soviet relations as it:

■ drained China's financial resources and therefore made it more dependent on the Soviet Union

■ demonstrated the courage and expertise of Chinese troops, thus persuading Stalin that China was a useful ally.

Consequently, the Korean War helped to consolidate the Sino-Soviet relationship.

Complete the Venn diagram

Use the information on the opposite page to add detail to the Venn diagram below. In the two main areas of the diagram, list the causes of the Sino-Soviet Treaty of Friendship relating only to the motives of China or the Soviet Union. In the intersecting area of the diagram, note ways in which these motives overlapped.

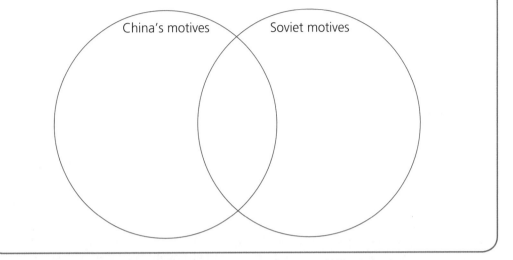

China's motives   Soviet motives

Eliminate irrelevance

a

Below are a sample exam-style question and a paragraph written in answer to this question. Read the paragraph and identify parts of the paragraph that are not directly relevant to the question. Draw a line through the information that is irrelevant and justify your deletions in the margin.

How accurate is it to say that ideology was the main reason for the signing of the Sino-Soviet Treaty of Friendship, Alliance and Mutual Assistance in 1950?

Ideology was one reason for the signing of the Sino-Soviet Treaty of Friendship, Alliance and Mutual Assistance in 1950. Both the Soviet Union and the People's Republic of China were communist powers. North Korea was also a communist power. This meant that they had a common hatred of capitalism, a common desire to spread equality, and a common commitment to economic development through planning. Their mutual commitment to communism meant that they had common enemies in the capitalist world, specifically the US and its ally Britain. This was not the first time that countries had allied due to fear of a common enemy. For example, during the Second World War, Britain, the US and the Soviet Union formed the Grand Alliance in order to combat the Axis Powers. In this way, ideology was one reason for the signing of the Sino-Soviet Treaty because the two sides were united in common objectives and against common enemies.

Sino-Soviet relations from 1956: evidence of deterioration

Sino-Soviet relations after Stalin

In the first years following Stalin's death in 1953 the relationship between the Soviet Union and China seemed to improve:

- The Soviet Union increased the amount of technical support it offered to China. With Soviet help, 116 fully equipped industrial plants were constructed. In particular, there was aid for producing metal, prospecting for oil, the development of machine tools and the manufacture of locomotives.
- 8000 Chinese students were invited onto advanced training courses in the Soviet Union.

Diplomatically, Khrushchev appeared to be more accommodating than Stalin. He signed an agreement to give up Soviet territory in Lushun and there seemed to be a positive working relationship between the Soviet Union and China at the **Geneva Conference of 1954.**

Deterioration of the Sino-Soviet relationship

In spite of Khrushchev's generosity there were important areas of difficulty between the two communist powers.

Personal mistrust

Mao had little respect for Khrushchev. While he respected Stalin as a courageous revolutionary, he believed that Khrushchev was nothing more than a timid **bureaucrat**. Mao's doubts about Khrushchev deepened when Khrushchev accused Stalin of betraying the Revolution in his Secret Speech of 1956 (see page 28). Khrushchev criticised Stalin for creating a '**cult of personality**', which concerned Mao who had created his own personality cult. Following the speech, Mao argued that Khrushchev was a dangerous **revisionist**.

Tension over Taiwan

Mao believed that in order to fully liberate China he needed to gain control of **Taiwan**, the geographical base of his nationalist opponents. Mao was frustrated by Khrushchev's refusal to support this.

Taiwan Crisis, 1954–1955

In 1954 Mao began to bomb Taiwan. The US quickly signed a Mutual Defence Treaty. In effect, this meant that the US would defend Taiwan against Chinese or Soviet attack. In public, Khrushchev supported China, but privately he was clear that he did not want to jeopardise **peaceful coexistence** with the US.

Taiwan Crisis, 1958

Aware of Mao's ambitions, the US provided **matador missiles** to defend Taiwan. In response, Mao bombarded **Quemoy and Matsu** in August 1958 as a means of stepping up pressure on the US. As tension mounted, Khrushchev refused to support China. Consequently, China was forced to back down.

The two Taiwan crises showed that Khrushchev was unwilling to support Mao's attempts to conquer Taiwan. Consequently, they deepened Mao's mistrust of Khrushchev.

Nuclear weapons

The Soviet Union and China were also divided on the issue of nuclear weapons:

- Khrushchev was alarmed by Mao's attitude to nuclear war: Mao stated that he was willing to see half the world's population die in order to advance **communism**.
- Mao viewed Khrushchev's commitment to 'peaceful coexistence' between **capitalism** and communism as a sign that Khrushchev was a coward who was betraying communism.

Khrushchev was horrified by Mao's willingness to use nuclear weapons and therefore refused to help China develop its own nuclear weapons. Mao felt betrayed. As an alternative, Khrushchev proposed the establishment of a sophisticated radio station in China, which would monitor US submarines in the Pacific. Mao took this as a patronising gesture – part of what he believed was a **cat and mouse relationship** on the part of the Soviets.

Below are a sample exam-style question and a paragraph written in answer to this question. Why does this paragraph not get into Level 4? Once you have identified the mistake, rewrite the paragraph so that it displays the qualities of Level 4. The mark scheme on page 109 will help you.

Why did Sino-Soviet relations deteriorate in the period 1953–1956?

> The change of leadership from Stalin to Khrushchev led to a significant decline in Sino-Soviet relations in the period 1953–1956. Mao's relationship with Stalin was strong because Mao respected Stalin as a true revolutionary. Therefore, in the period 1949–1953 the Sino-Soviet relationship was strong and stable. Evidence of this is found in the Treaty of Friendship signed by the Soviet Union and China in 1950. However, following Stalin's death in 1953, a new leadership team emerged. By 1956, Khrushchev was the undisputed leader of the Soviet Union. Mao believed that Khrushchev was not a true revolutionary. Rather, he thought Khrushchev was a timid bureaucrat and, in ideological terms, a dangerous revisionist.

Below are a sample exam-style question and a paragraph written in answer to this question. The paragraph contains a point and a concluding explanatory link back to the question, but lacks examples. Complete the paragraph adding examples in the space provided.

Why did Sino-Soviet relations deteriorate in the period 1953–1956?

> Disagreements between the Soviet Union and China over Taiwan were a further reason for the deterioration of Sino-Soviet relations in the period 1953–1956. For example,
>
> _____
>
> _____
>
> _____
>
> _____
>
> In this way, tensions over Taiwan were a clear reason for the deterioration of the Sino-Soviet relationship because Mao felt betrayed by Khrushchev and unable to rely on him for further support.

Ideological rivals, 1958–1966

China's new direction

In 1958, Mao launched the **Great Leap Forward**, an economic policy that he claimed was superior to the Soviet economic model. Khrushchev was frustrated by the implicit criticism of Soviet policy. The new policy reflected growing ideological differences between China and the Soviet Union. Mao felt that Khrushchev's style of government had become bureaucratic, and he wanted Chinese communism to maintain its radical spirit. Therefore, his new policy was based on the creative power of China's peasants over the technical expertise of Soviet advisors.

Significantly, the new policy reflected Mao's increasing self-confidence and his desire to replace Khrushchev as leader of the communist world. Khrushchev understood this and criticised Mao's new policies, creating greater strain between the two leaders. In 1960, the tensions came to the surface when Khrushchev ordered the removal of all 1390 Soviet experts from China and the cancellation of all 257 joint technical projects.

Mao's new policy was a spectacular failure, and resulted in a major famine. However, Sino-Soviet relations had deteriorated to such an extent that Mao refused Soviet offers of emergency supplies of grain and sugar.

Public dispute

During 1963, the Soviet Communist Party and the Chinese Communist Party criticised each other more formally. The *Open Letter of the Communist Party of the Soviet Union* argued that China was no longer on the true path to communism. Mao responded with even greater criticism, arguing that the Soviet Union had re-established capitalism. Mao's refusal to compromise with the Soviet Union was based, in part, on a genuine ideological rejection of bureaucracy, which he regarded as a central part of '**Soviet revisionism**'.

Moscow meeting, 1964

Following Khrushchev's fall, the new Soviet leadership of Leonid Brezhnev and Alexei Kosygin held talks in Moscow with Zhou Enlai, China's Foreign Minister, during the celebrations of the 47th anniversary of the **Russian Revolution**. However, the talks were unsuccessful. China was increasingly unwilling to compromise as:

■ it had successfully tested a nuclear device and, as a consequence, had less need of Soviet protection

■ communist Albania had rejected Soviet leadership and allied with China.

The Soviet government was also inflexible. Indeed, powerful figures in the Soviet government felt that Mao would soon be ousted, just as Khrushchev had been removed as Soviet leader. The Soviet Defence Minister, Marshal Malinovsky, went as far as to suggest a leadership change to Chinese diplomats. With no sign of compromise on either side the talks broke down.

Chinese domestic politics

Chinese domestic politics was another factor that led to a breakdown in Sino-Soviet relations. Since the failure of the Great Leap Forward, Mao had been forced to play a smaller role in government. By the mid-1960s, Mao was determined to reassert his authority and eliminate his rivals. Consequently, in 1966, he launched the **Cultural Revolution**, which was designed to purge 'Soviet revisionists' from the Chinese government. During the Cultural Revolution, Mao's anti-Soviet rhetoric intensified. Indeed, Liu Shaoqi, Mao's main rival, was publicly denounced as the 'Chinese Khrushchev'. Mobs of student activists besieged the Soviet embassy in Beijing and Foreign Minister Zhou Enlai had to intervene to prevent it being burnt down.

Support or challenge?

Below is a sample exam-style question which asks how far you agree with a specific statement. Below this is a series of general statements which are relevant to the question. Using your own knowledge and the information on the opposite page decide whether these statements support or challenge the statement in the question and tick the appropriate box.

'By 1964, Sino-Soviet relations had broken down.' How far do you agree with this opinion?

	SUPPORT	CHALLENGE
The Soviet Union refused to support China during the Taiwan Crises of 1954 and 1958.		
The Great Leap Forward was an implicit criticism of Soviet economic policy.		
Khrushchev offered economic aid to China following the failure of the Great Leap Forward.		
In 1963, the Soviet Union published the *Open Letter.*		
Mao never fully trusted Khrushchev.		
Khrushchev was removed as Soviet leader during 1964.		
Brezhnev and Kosygin held talks with Zhou Enlai in 1964.		
Marshal Malinovsky suggested that the Chinese government needed a new leader.		

Simple essay style

Below is a sample exam-style question. Use your own knowledge and the information on the opposite page to produce a plan for this question. Choose four general points, and provide three pieces of specific information to support each general point. Once you have planned your essay, write the introduction and conclusion for the essay. The introduction should list the points to be discussed in the essay. The conclusion should summarise the key points and justify which point was the most important.

How far was the deterioration in Sino-Soviet relations in the years 1953–1964 due to ideological differences?

The Sino-Soviet border conflict, 1969

Military confrontation

In 1969, the ideological disputes between the Soviet Union and China transformed into a military conflict. The conflict emerged over the 4406-kilometre Sino-Soviet border. There had been occasional border clashes since 1967, but Mao became more concerned about Soviet forces on the Sino-Soviet border during 1968. In August 1968, Brezhnev ordered Soviet troops into Czechoslovakia to overthrow the government. He argued that the Czechoslovakian government had left the path of true communism and therefore that the Soviet government had the right to replace them. Mao was afraid that the **Brezhnev doctrine** might apply to China and therefore that the Soviet government would claim the right to replace the Chinese government.

Fearing a Soviet attack, the Chinese built up their forces on the Sino-Soviet border. The Soviets, also fearing war, reacted by establishing a network of new **command centres** to repel a Chinese attack. The establishment of Soviet command centres convinced China that the Soviet Union was preparing for war. Consequently, China decided on a policy of 'active defence', which involved launching a pre-emptive attack. On 2 March 1969 Chinese troops ambushed a Soviet border patrol near Zhenbao Island in the Ussuri River region. The situation became fraught enough for the Soviet government to threaten a nuclear attack. Mao responded by hastily constructing nuclear shelters in Beijing.

Defusing the crisis

The border crisis was resolved in mid-September at a meeting between Chinese foreign minister Zhou and his Soviet equal, Kosygin, at Beijing Airport. The two sides gave assurance that they had no intention of invading and agreed to maintain the existing border and avoid military clashes.

The impact of the Sino-Soviet split on the Cold War

Initially, the Sino-Soviet split had no impact on the relationship between the US and the Soviet Union. Officials in the US government assumed that China and the Soviet Union were allies due to their common ideology. Indeed, there was little interest in the ideological disputes between the two communist nations at the top of the US government. The US's prime concern was containing communism in Vietnam (see page 56), and, significantly the Soviet Union and China continued to collaborate in order to supply communist troops in Vietnam with weaponry to fight US troops. However, by the late 1960s, the Sino-Soviet split had become public and therefore senior US officials began to discuss turning the Sino-Soviet split to their advantage.

The 1969 border conflict was significant as it forced the new US President **Richard Nixon** to consider the US's position regarding a Sino-Soviet military conflict. Nixon reached the view that a successful Soviet invasion of China would give the Soviet Union a new advantage in the **Cold War**, as it would allow the Soviet Union to dominate Asia. Consequently, Nixon asked his military chiefs to devise plans, including plans for using nuclear weapons, to prevent a Soviet takeover of China.

Below are a sample exam-style question and a list of general points which could be used to answer the question. Use your own knowledge and the information on the opposite page to reach a judgement about the importance of these general points to the question posed. Write numbers on the spectrum below to indicate their relative importance. Having done this, write a brief justification of your placement, explaining why some of these factors are more important than others. The resulting diagram could form the basis of an essay plan.

Why had tensions between the Soviet Union and the People's Republic of China developed into full-scale confrontation by 1969?

1. Ideological conflict between Mao and the Soviet leadership
2. Personal differences between Mao and the Soviet leadership
3. Mao's fear that the Brezhnev doctrine would apply to China

4. Khrushchev's decision not to share nuclear secrets with China
5. Disagreements over the status of Taiwan
6. Disputes over the Sino-Soviet border

Very important ←——————————————————→ Less important

Below are a simple introduction and conclusion for an essay in answer to the sample exam-style question in the 'Spectrum of significance' activity above. The general points in that activity also form a list of key points to be made in the essay. Read the question, the general points, and the introduction and conclusion. Rewrite the introduction and the conclusion in order to develop an argument.

Why had tensions between the Soviet Union and the People's Republic of China developed into full-scale confrontation by 1969?

Key points:

- Ideological conflict between Mao and the Soviet leadership
- Personal differences between Mao and the Soviet leadership
- Mao's fear that the Brezhnev doctrine would apply to China

- Khrushchev's decision not to share nuclear secrets with China
- Disagreements over the status of Taiwan
- Disputes over the Sino-Soviet border

Introduction

There were six key reasons why tensions between the Soviet Union and China developed into full-scale confrontation by 1969. These were ideological conflict between Mao and the Soviet leadership, personal differences between Mao and the Soviet leadership, Mao's fear that the Brezhnev doctrine would apply to China, Khrushchev's decision not to share nuclear secrets with China, disagreements over the status of Taiwan, and disputes over the Sino-Soviet border.

Conclusion

There were six key reasons why tensions between the Soviet Union and China developed into full-scale confrontation by 1969. All of these reasons were of equal importance.

Nixon and Mao

From 1949, successive US presidents refused to recognise or have any dealings with Mao's regime. Indeed, the US recognised the nationalist government in Taiwan as the official government of China and blocked communist China from gaining membership of the **United Nations**. Chinese involvement in Korea (see page 18) had increased the antagonism. Furthermore, China officially reviled the US, whom they named 'Number One Enemy'.

Why did the US move closer to China?

This situation changed in the early 1970s under the Republican president Richard Nixon. Nixon had a variety of reasons for wanting closer links with China:

- Nixon wanted to end US involvement in the **Vietnam War**. However, he did not want the US to be humiliated. He felt that Mao would be able to put pressure on communist North Vietnam to negotiate with the US, and to achieve this he would have to establish relations with Mao's regime.
- China's relationship with the Soviet Union had broken down. Nixon hoped that closer ties between the US and China would further weaken the Soviet Union's international position while strengthening the position of the US.
- Nixon hoped to be able to moderate China's influence and thereby stop the spread of communism in Asia.
- Nixon was worried by the prospect of a Sino-Soviet war, fearing that it would lead to a Soviet victory and therefore Soviet dominance across the whole of Asia.
- The Vietnam War had demonstrated the limits of US military power. Therefore, Nixon wanted to bolster the position of the US through new strategic alliances.
- Nixon hoped that a better relationship with China would allow the US to focus its entire **nuclear arsenal** on the Soviet Union.

Why did China move closer to the US?

Mao also had a variety of reasons for wanting closer links with the US. First, he was concerned about China's **geopolitical** position:

- There were still tensions between China and the Soviet Union over their joint border, and Mao was worried about a pre-emptive Soviet nuclear attack.
- Mao was concerned that China was encircled by unfriendly states. He stated, 'We have the Soviet Union to the north and west; India to the south and Japan to the east'.
- China's relationship with India had become increasingly hostile. Indeed, the two countries had been at war in 1962 and there was significant conflict in 1967. Furthermore, Mao had become increasingly concerned by the Soviet Union's public support for India.

There were also economic factors:

- The leaders of the Chinese petroleum industry argued that their resources were in need of investment and research. The US was the undisputed world leader in petroleum technology. Consequently, China sought better links with the US in the hope of gaining support for its industry.

Pragmatism

Essentially, better relations between the two countries were possible because Mao and Nixon were prepared to act pragmatically: to put aside ideological conflict in favour of a relationship based on mutual economic and strategic interests.

Develop the detail

Below is a sample exam-style question and a paragraph written in answer to this question. The paragraph contains a limited amount of detail. Annotate the paragraph to add additional detail to the answer.

Why did the US pursue closer relations with the People's Republic of China in the period 1969–1970?

One reason why the US pursued closer relations with China in the period 1969–1970 was the belief that the US and China had areas of common interest. Nixon was aware of the deterioration in Sino-Soviet relations. Specifically, he was aware of the recent border conflict that had brought the Soviet Union and China to the brink of war. Therefore, Nixon was aware that the two countries shared a common enemy. Nixon hoped that an understanding between the two nations would put the Soviet Union under pressure. In this way, a belief in a shared interest between China and the US was one reason why the US pursued closer relations with China because Nixon hoped to exploit common feelings of animosity towards the Soviet Union and turn these to the advantage of the US.

Developing an argument

Below is a sample exam-style question, a list of key points to be made in the essay, and a paragraph from the essay. Read the question, the plan and the sample paragraph. Rewrite the paragraph in order to develop an argument. Your paragraph should explain why the factor discussed in the paragraph is either more or less significant than the factor mentioned in the question.

How far was Nixon's desire to end the Vietnam War the main reason why the US decided to pursue closer relations with the People's Republic of China in the period 1969–1970?

Key points:

- The belief that the US and China had areas of common interest.
- Nixon desired to end the Vietnam War.
- Nixon feared a Sino-Soviet war.
- Nixon hoped to stop the spread of communism in Asia.

Sample paragraph

Nixon's fear of a Sino-Soviet war was one reason why the US decided to pursue closer relations with China in the period 1969–1970. Nixon was aware that the Sino-Soviet border conflict of 1969, which escalated from a conflict near the Zhenbao Island in the Ussuri River region, had taken the Soviet Union and China to the brink of war. By 1969, both the Soviet Union and China were nuclear powers and therefore any Sino-Soviet war was likely to escalate into a nuclear conflict. By 1969, the Soviet Union had the second largest nuclear arsenal in the world. Any war between the Soviet Union and China would therefore end in Soviet victory and Nixon was concerned that a Sino-Soviet war would lead to Soviet domination of the entire continent of Asia. Therefore, Nixon decided to pursue closer relations with China in order to deter a Soviet invasion and consequently to prevent Soviet domination of Asia.

Nixon in China

'Ping-pong diplomacy'

Between 1969 and 1972 China and the US developed a closer relationship:

- In 1969 Nixon began secret talks with China.
- In January 1970, the Chinese and US ambassadors to Poland met. The Chinese ambassador said that China wanted to arrange talks 'at a high level' between the two countries.
- In early April 1971, the Chinese and the US ping-pong teams met during a tournament in Japan. As a result the US team were invited to China to enjoy 'Friendship First, Competition Second'. The US team visited Beijing in mid-April. As a result, steps towards a new Sino-US relationship became known as 'ping-pong diplomacy'.
- In late 1971, US National Security Advisor Henry Kissinger secretly visited Beijing for talks with Zhou. The two agreed that Nixon would visit China in 1972.

'The week that changed the world'

Nixon travelled to China in February 1972, describing his trip as 'the week that changed the world'. The trip culminated in a meeting between the two leaders. The summit between the two leaders was a clear indication that the **bi-polar world**, dominated by two superpowers, was at an end and that China was now a significant world power.

The meeting did not lead to a formal Sino-US alliance, but it was clearly successful. As a result of the meeting, China began to downplay its support for the 'revolutionary struggle' in the **Third World** and both powers released a statement condemning 'Soviet Imperialism'.

The Shanghai Communiqué

Nixon's visit concluded with the publication of a joint communiqué setting out the basic agreement that had been drawn up by Kissinger and Zhou.

The Shanghai Communiqué set out the following principles:

- No single power should attempt to dominate Asia. This aspect of the communiqué was a tacit warning that the US would not tolerate a Soviet invasion of China.
- The US and China should develop closer cultural and educational links. Trade between the two nations developed from 5 million dollars in 1972 to 500 million dollars within the decade.

In addition to these joint principles, the US acknowledged that Taiwan was part of China.

The impact on the Soviet Union

Nixon's visit to China and the Shanghai Communiqué horrified Soviet leaders. As Nixon hoped, the fear of a Sino-US alliance forced Soviet leaders to cultivate a better relationship with the US. This was reflected in the Moscow Summit of May 1972 (see page 62).

At the same time, Soviet leaders began to prepare for a 'war on two fronts', against the US in the west and China in the east. This forced the Soviet Union to divide its forces, and therefore diminished their effectiveness.

Sino-US relations, 1973–1976

Nixon's successor, **Gerald Ford**, continued to try to build a close relationship with China. Consequently, during 1975, Kissinger and Ford both visited China. However, due to the impact of the **Watergate Scandal**, Ford was in a weaker position than Nixon. He had assumed the presidency following Nixon's resignation. Therefore he had not been elected president, and could not claim to represent the people. Consequently, he was not able to compromise on important issues, and the meetings consolidated the link between the two powers, rather than leading to full **normalisation** of the Sino-US relationship.

RAG – Rate the timeline

Below are a sample exam-style question and a timeline. Read the question, study the timeline and, using three coloured pens, put a Red, Amber or Green star next to the events to show:

Red: Events and policies that have no relevance to the question
Amber: Events and policies that have some significance to the question
Green: Events and policies that are directly relevant to the question

1) Why did the Sino-Soviet relationship deteriorate in the years 1955–1969?

Now repeat the activity with the following questions:

2) How far did the Sino-Soviet relationship deteriorate in the period 1955–1969?

3) How far did Sino-Soviet relations improve in the period 1969–1975?

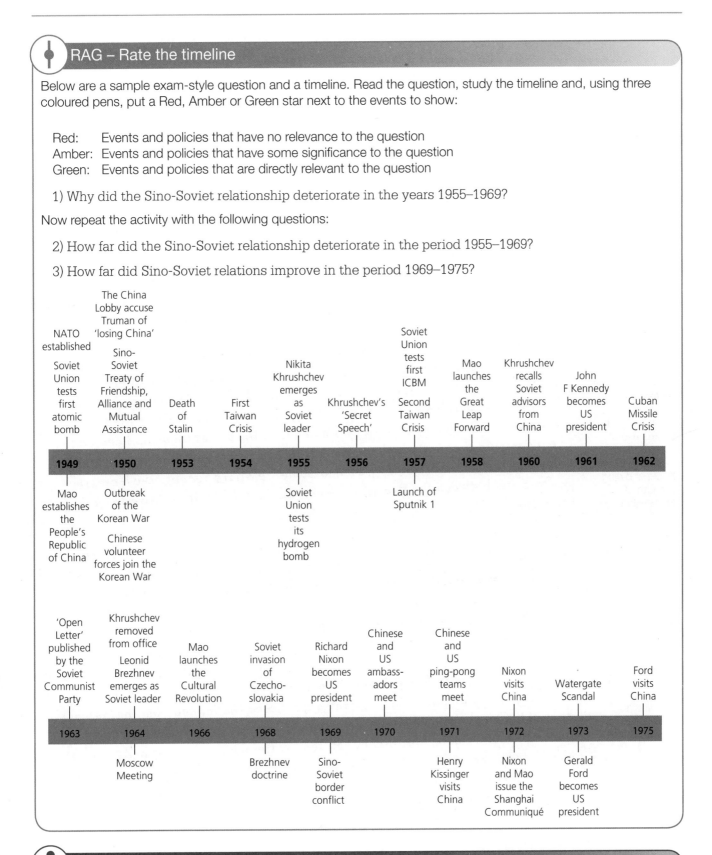

Recommended reading

Below is a list of suggested further reading on this topic.

- *The Sino-Soviet Split,* chapter 2, Lorenz M Luthi (2010)
- *Nixon's China Trip*, chapter 9, Eric J Ladley (2002)

Exam focus

Below is a sample A grade Part (a) essay. Read it and the examiner comments around it.

'The breakdown in Sino-Soviet relations was primarily due to ideological differences.' How far do you agree with this view? (30 marks)

The introduction focuses on the question and outlines the factors that will be discussed in the essay.

Ideology clearly played an important role in the breakdown of Sino-Soviet relations. However, the differing national interests of the two countries were also a cause of conflict, as was rivalry between the two powers, and personal disputes, particularly between Mao and Khrushchev.

The essay begins with a paragraph that focuses on the factor stated in the question. This shows an immediate focus on the question. In addition, this paragraph makes use of material from Section 5 of this book, showing breadth of knowledge.

Ideological differences undoubtedly pushed the two powers apart, particularly in the late 1950s and 1960s. The difference between Soviet communism and Mao's understanding of communism became particularly clear in 1958 with the launch of Mao's Great Leap Forward. Mao felt that Soviet economic planning had lost its revolutionary spirit. By contrast, Mao argued that the Great Leap Forward was ideologically superior as it was based on the creative power of China's peasants. Ideological disputes came to a head in 1963. The Soviet Communist Party published its 'Open Letter', which argued that China had left the true path of communism. Mao responded by arguing that the Soviet Union had ceased to be a communist country and had re-established capitalism. Evidently, ideology played a part in the breakdown of Sino-Soviet relations because the increasing differences between the two governments made it difficult for them to work together.

This paragraph shows detailed knowledge of the period by mentioning both of the Taiwan Crises.

However, the two powers were also divided by their different national interests. Mao's key strategic goal was to capture Taiwan. The Soviet government refused to support Mao's campaign. Divisions over Taiwan first emerged in 1954 when China bombed the island. The US quickly allied with Taiwan. Mao hoped to have Soviet support, but the Soviet government was pursuing 'peaceful coexistence' with the US and therefore was unwilling to commit military support. The Soviet government believed that 'peaceful coexistence' was in the Soviet national interest as it would allow the Soviet Union to reduce military spending and therefore divert resources to raising living standards. Mao, by contrast, believed that conquering Taiwan was crucial to China's national interest. The second Taiwan Crisis of 1958 resulted in similar divisions. Again, Khrushchev refused to offer military support and Mao was humiliated by being forced to back down. In this way, the differences in national interest were clearly one reason for the breakdown in Sino-Soviet relations because in key areas both countries were more committed to seeking their own national interest than they were to co-operating.

This paragraph shows a range of knowledge as it covers the period from 1949 to 1964.

A third factor that caused the breakdown in Sino-Soviet relations was rivalry for leadership of the communist world. In the period 1949 to 1953, Mao accepted Stalin as the leader of world communism. Mao respected Stalin and this was reflected in the Treaty of Friendship, Alliance and Mutual Assistance, which explicitly acknowledged Soviet superiority. However, by the late 1950s Mao had much less respect for the leadership of the Soviet Union. Mao believed that the new Soviet policy of 'peaceful coexistence' was a sign that the new

Soviet leadership were betraying world communism. Moreover, Mao felt that Khrushchev's refusal to share Soviet nuclear secrets with China was another sign that the new Soviet leadership were no longer willing to fight capitalism. By 1964, China had showed a willingness to act independently by launching the Great Leap Forward, successfully testing its first nuclear bomb, and winning Albania as an ally. Therefore, Mao saw himself as the true leader of the communist world. This rivalry to be seen as the leader of world communism led to a breakdown in Sino-Soviet relations because it created distrust and conflict between the leaders of the two communist countries.

Finally, personalities also played a role in the breakdown in Sino-Soviet relations. Mao had very little respect for Khrushchev, and Khrushchev grew increasingly frustrated by Mao. For Mao, Stalin deserved respect for he was a true and courageous revolutionary. However, Mao believed that Khrushchev was nothing more than a cowardly bureaucrat. Mao believed that Khrushchev had shown his timidity over Taiwan and again on the issue of nuclear weapons. Khrushchev thought Mao was extremely unwise. Mao's biggest policy initiative had ended in a devastating famine and Khrushchev was concerned that Mao was too willing to launch a nuclear war. Mao also thought that Khrushchev's offers of aid during the famine and Khrushchev's desire to establish military bases in China were part of a patronising attitude towards China on the part of the Soviet leadership. Distrust continued following Khrushchev's fall from power. In 1968 Brezhnev invaded Czechoslovakia in order to remove a communist government that was no longer willing to take orders from the Soviet Union. Therefore, during the border conflict Mao feared that Brezhnev would do the same to China. The personal distrust was clearly a big part of the breakdown of Sino-Soviet relations because it meant that the leaders of the two countries could not work together.

In conclusion, personal conflict played a more important role in the breakdown of Sino-Soviet relations than other factors. This is evident from the fact that there were strategic differences, ideological differences and rivalries between the Soviet Union and China from the beginning of the relationship. Nonetheless, Mao's respect for Stalin meant that the two countries could collaborate extremely effectively. Mao's mistrust of Khrushchev and then Brezhnev heightened the existing tensions, including ideological differences, leading to a breakdown in relations.

The paragraph finishes with a clear analytical link to the question, explaining why personal differences played a key role in the breakdown in Sino-Soviet relations.

Rather than just summarising the essay, the conclusion presents an argument about the relative importance of the different factors. Had this argument been integrated into the rest of the essay, it could have achieved a mark in Level 5.

24/30

This essay is awarded a mark in Level 4 as it focuses clearly on the question, provides detailed examples to support its points, and links back to the question with an analytical statement at the end of each paragraph. However, the essay cannot be awarded a mark within Level 5 because it does not contain sustained analysis. Although an argument is stated in the conclusion, this is not sustained throughout the essay.

Moving from Level 4 to Level 5

The Exam Focus at the end of Section 2 provided a Level 5 essay. The essay here achieves a Level 4. Read both essays, and the examiner's comments provided. Make a list of the additional features required to push a Level 4 essay into Level 5.

Section 5: *Détente*, 1969–1980

The origins of *détente*

Détente refers to a relaxation in tension between the two **superpowers**. It was the result of a deliberate attempt to avoid the crises that had characterised the **Cold War** to date.

The origins of *détente*

The Soviet perspective

Leonid Brezhnev had played a key role in the removal of Khrushchev in 1964. During the late 1960s he emerged as Soviet leader. Brezhnev sought a better relationship with the US for the following reasons:

- The **Soviet Union** had achieved **relative nuclear parity** in armaments and therefore felt it could negotiate from a position of strength.
- The Soviet Union was experiencing economic problems. Its economy was roughly one-sixth the size of the US economy. Soviet leaders wanted to boost economic growth and living standards by reducing military spending.
- Soviet leaders wanted to buy cheap grain from the West.
- Soviet leaders wanted access to superior Western technology.
- Soviet relations with China had deteriorated and this weakened the strength of the communist bloc.

The US perspective

Richard Nixon became US president in January 1969. He was a well-known opponent of **communism**. Nonetheless, Nixon was a **realist** and felt the Cold War was draining US resources. He believed that the US should seek a more stable relationship with the Soviet Union. He sought *détente* for the following reasons:

- US leaders wanted to end the **Vietnam War**. They hoped that improved relations with the Soviet Union would result in decreased Soviet support for communist North Vietnam.
- The US economy was beginning to stagnate. US leaders wanted to reduce defence spending in order to promote economic growth through trade with the Soviet Union and Eastern Europe.

The Moscow Summit, 1972

The Moscow Summit of 1972 was one of the first successes of *détente*. It led to two agreements.

SALT 1

The Strategic Arms Limitation Treaty (SALT 1) comprised the following:

- The Anti-Ballistic Missile Treaty allowed each superpower to deploy only two **Anti-Ballistic Missile Shields (ABMS)**. Both sides recognised that ABMS undermined the possibility of **mutually assured destruction (MAD)** because ABMS had the potential to neutralise nuclear missile attacks. Additionally, as the US was technologically more advanced, it was more likely that the US would develop an effective ABMS ahead of the Soviet Union. This made nuclear war more likely because, with an effective ABMS, the US could attack the Soviet Union without threat of retaliation.
- The Interim Agreement on Offensive Missiles placed limits on ICBMs and submarine-launched missiles. This allowed the Soviet Union a 3:2 advantage in ICBMs, but it in turn agreed to allow the US to continue to station shorter-range weapons in Western Europe. The agreement was designed to last five years in the hope that a permanent treaty could be drawn up by 1977.

SALT 1 was recognised as a temporary measure and led immediately to discussions for a permanent treaty, which would be known as SALT 2.

The Basic Principles Agreement

The agreement set out twelve basic principles designed to govern superpower relations. For example, both sides, and their allies, agreed to respect each other as equals, to accept peaceful coexistence, to seek disarmament, to increase trade and to avoid confrontation.

The significance of the Moscow Summit

The Moscow Summit was significant because it showed that the leaders of the two superpowers were committed to working together. Additionally, the Basic Principles Agreement established, for the first time, a framework governing superpower relations.

Complete the paragraph ⓐ

Below are a sample exam-style question and a paragraph written in answer to this question. The paragraph contains a point and a concluding explanatory link back to the question, but lacks examples. Complete the paragraph, adding examples in the space provided.

How far did superpower tensions relax in the period 1969–1980?

> Superpower tensions clearly relaxed as a result of the Moscow Summit of 1972. For example,
>
> _____
>
> _____
>
> _____
>
> _____
>
> In this way, superpower tensions clearly relaxed as a result of the Moscow Summit as it led to arms limitation and a degree of normalisation in superpower relations.

Complete the Venn diagram

Use the information that you have gained so far to add detail to the Venn diagram below. Use the diagram to illustrate the motives of *détente* specific to each of the two superpowers, and the motives that were common to both.

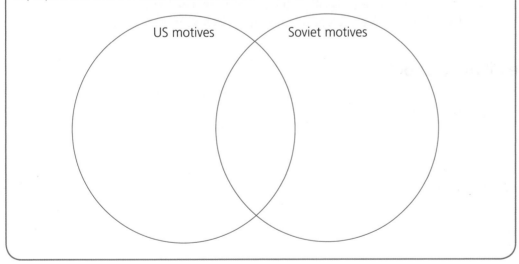

The oil price shock

The OPEC Crisis

The 1973 **OPEC** economic crisis threatened to alter the balance of power in the Cold War. In October 1973, OPEC, the Organisation of Petroleum Exporting Countries, refused to supply oil to Israel's allies in response to the **Yom Kippur War**. This led to a quadrupling of the international price of oil.

The impact on the Cold War

The OPEC Crisis had different implications for the two superpowers.

- In the West, the Crisis created an oil shortage. This led to an atmosphere of crisis in the US as US economic growth relied on cheap oil. Additionally, the OPEC Crisis threatened car and **freeway** use, which for many Americans was a crucial part of the national way of life. In a sense, the OPEC Crisis and continuing problems related to the Vietnam War led to a feeling that the US was in decline and losing ground against communism in the Cold War.

- The Crisis benefited the Soviet Union because it was an oil-exporting state. Therefore, the money that the Soviet Union raised by selling oil could be used to buy US grain and technology. Increased oil revenues held out the prospect of reversing Soviet economic decline.

Western recovery

In spite of fears in the US, the major Western economies quickly rebounded. This occurred for the following reasons:

- Economic co-ordination: the creation of the **G7**, a committee of the finance ministers of the seven largest Western economies, in 1975 allowed Western governments to co-operate more easily on economic issues. This restored confidence to international financial markets and restored economic stability after the oil price shock.

- Technical innovation: Western companies began to develop more fuel-efficient engines, which meant that they needed to import less oil.

- Renewed oil price stability: the Crisis was relatively short-lived. Between 1974 and 1978 the price of oil remained stable and therefore confidence and growth returned to Western economies.

The impact of the oil price shock

The oil price shock led to a widespread perception, particularly on the **right wing** of US politics, that the US was vulnerable and doing too little to safeguard its position in the world. This feeling led to further criticisms of *détente*, and demands for a more assertive foreign policy that would re-establish the confidence of the US.

Additionally, the OPEC Crisis emphasised the importance of safeguarding oil reserves. This turned the attention of US leaders to the Middle East, an oil-rich region of the world. As a result, US leaders were extremely concerned about any expansion of Soviet influence in the Middle East as they feared it might lead to another oil crisis.

Simple essay style

Below is a sample exam-style question. Use your own knowledge and the information on the opposite page to produce a plan for this question. Choose four general points, and provide three pieces of specific information to support each general point. Once you have planned your essay, write the introduction and conclusion for the essay. The introduction should list the points to be discussed in the essay. The conclusion should summarise the key points and justify which point was the most important.

How far did the oil price shock of 1973 destabilise *détente* between the superpowers?

Identify an argument (a)

Below are a series of definitions, a sample exam-style question and two sample conclusions. One of the conclusions achieves a high level because it contains an argument. The other achieves a lower level because it contains only a description and assertion. Identify which is which. The mark scheme on page 109 will help you.

Description: a detailed account.
Assertion: a statement of fact or an opinion that is not supported by a reason.
Reason: a statement that explains or justifies something.
Argument: an assertion justified with a reason.

How successful was *détente* in relaxing superpower relations by 1975?

Sample 1

In conclusion, détente was partially successful in relaxing superpower tensions by 1975 because the initial success of the Moscow Summit proved impossible to sustain due to the economic problems caused by the OPEC Crisis of 1973. Consequently, US leaders were less willing to negotiate with the Soviet Union following the OPEC Crisis because, in the short term, the OPEC Crisis seemed to give the Soviet Union an economic advantage in the Cold War.

Sample 2

In conclusion, détente was partially successful in relaxing superpower tensions by 1975. Nixon pursued détente in order to solve US economic problems and in an attempt to end the Vietnam War. The Soviet Union pursued détente because it believed that it could negotiate with the West from a position of strength and because relations between the Soviet Union and China had deteriorated.

The Helsinki Accords, 1975

Ostpolitik

Movement towards *détente* did not only come from the superpowers. There were also developments and initiatives in Europe. One of the most significant of these was the policy of **Ostpolitik**, which was advanced by the West German leader Willy Brandt and designed to improve relationships between **NATO** and the **Warsaw Pact** countries.

The origins of *Ostpolitik*

The underlying objective of West German leaders was the reunification of Germany. In 1969, a new government was formed in West Germany under the leadership of Willy Brandt. Brandt felt that contact with the **Eastern bloc** was the best way to establish and stabilise relations. He signed the **Treaty of Moscow** (1970) and the Basic Principles Treaty (1972). In so doing, he accepted the existing borders between East and West Germany. For Brandt, this was the first stage in a dialogue with East Germany that he hoped would lead to reunification.

Ostpolitik and Eastern Europe

Eastern bloc countries welcomed *Ostpolitik* for two reasons:

■ It would help improve trading relations with the West.

■ It would give them access to Western technology.

The Helsinki Accords, 1975

Improving relations between Eastern and Western Europe led to the Helsinki Accords. The Accords were issued following an international conference involving 33 countries, including the Soviet Union. The conference focused on security and co-operation in Europe.

The Accords reflected agreements in three key areas, which were referred to as 'baskets':

Basket 1	This contained the Soviet Union's key objective. The Soviet Union gained acceptance of the frontiers of Europe as established in the settlements at the end of the Second World War. In other words, all European nations recognised the Soviet bloc.
Basket 2	This involved trade and technology exchanges. All nations agreed to expand trade and share technology.
Basket 3	This contained the key objective of the West. It committed all the signatories to respect human rights. This aspect of the treaty was unenforceable. Therefore, it was criticised because it was unlikely to improve the human rights situation in communist countries.

The significance of the Helsinki Accords

US politicians, such as **Ronald Reagan**, criticised the Helsinki Accords for compromising too much with the Soviet Union. However, in the long run, the Accords undermined the legitimacy of communism in the Eastern bloc:

■ Basket 2 allowed greater trade and gave communist countries access to Western technology. The superiority of Western technology implicitly undermined official claims that communism was a better system than **capitalism**.

■ Greater trade also allowed Western businesspeople to travel more freely to the East. Through informal contact with Western businesspeople, citizens of Eastern European countries learnt about Western press freedom and political democracy. This encouraged them to question the repressive and undemocratic nature of communist government.

■ Basket 3 played a part in undermining the hold of the repressive regimes in Eastern Europe. Andrei Sakharov, a campaigner in the Soviet Union, said that it 'gave human rights groups in the Soviet Union an anchor in International Law'. Sakharov founded the Moscow Helsinki Group to monitor and publicise human rights abuses. The emergence of popular movements for political freedom and economic and social advance would play a significant part in the subsequent collapse of Soviet rule. Later, US politicians would also criticise the Soviet Union for failing to keep to the terms of this basket.

Spot the mistake

Below are a sample exam-style question and a paragraph written in answer to this question. Why does this paragraph not get into Level 4? Once you have identified the mistake, rewrite the paragraph so that it displays the qualities of Level 4. The mark scheme on page 109 will help you.

How accurate is it to say that the Helsinki Accords had an unlooked-for significance for the Soviet Union and the Eastern bloc?

> The Helsinki Accords came about because of détente. At the end of the 1960s, both the Soviet Union and the US decided to pursue a policy of relaxation of superpower relations. This policy, which was known as détente in the US, came about due to the fact that President Nixon was a 'realist'. This meant that he believed that superpower relations could be based on common interest, rather than ideological conflict. At the same time, Leonid Brezhnev, the Soviet leader, sought a better relationship with the US in order to obtain superior Western technology and cheap supplies of grain.

Eliminate irrelevance

Below are a sample exam-style question and a paragraph written in answer to this question. Read the paragraph and identify parts of the paragraph that are not directly relevant to the question. Draw a line through the information that is irrelevant and justify your deletions in the margin.

How far did *détente* stabilise superpower relations in the period 1969–1975?

> The Helsinki Accords of 1975 certainly helped stabilise superpower relations. The Helsinki Accords were part of a broader policy known as Ostpolitik, which was initiated by the German leader Willy Brandt. Brandt was keen to pursue Ostpolitik because of his commitment to the reunification of Germany. The Helsinki Accords helped stabilise superpower relations by agreeing foundations for three key areas of East–West relations. Basket 1 of the Helsinki Accords agreed borders between East and West, Basket 2 opened the door to more trade, particularly in technology, and Basket 3 contained a commitment to respect human rights. However, the Helsinki Accords did not wholly stabilise superpower relations as US politicians, such as Ronald Reagan, criticised the Soviet Union and the US policy of détente by arguing that the Soviet Union and its Eastern European allies were not observing the terms of Basket 3. Reagan later initiated the SDI programme, which some historians believe was crucial in ending the Cold War. In this way, the Helsinki Accords partially stabilised superpower relations by agreeing a framework for East–West relations, but also undermined the stability of superpower relations by allowing right-wing US politicians to criticise détente.

How successful was *détente*, 1969–1976?

By 1976, the results of *détente* were clearly mixed.

SALT 2 negotiations

After the success of SALT 1, further arms control proved difficult to achieve. SALT 2 negotiations were protracted and difficult, and by 1976, the terms of the treaty were still being discussed.

- The US's allies in Europe were concerned about the deployment of the Soviet **SS20** medium-range missile. The West Germans, in particular, were worried that US arms reduction would leave Germany poorly defended.

- There was resistance in the US **Congress**. For example, Congressman Henry 'Scoop' Jackson argued that the Soviet Union would use the treaty to slow US arms production in order to overtake the US in terms of military might.

- The **Watergate Scandal**, which led to Nixon's resignation, sapped the authority of the US government, weakening its negotiating position at the Vladivostok Summit of 1974. Nonetheless, the Vladivostok Agreement of 1974 set out the basis for further negotiations: both sides agreed to equal limits for missile launchers and strategic bombers. However, the Vladivostok Agreement fell short of a full treaty, and SALT 2 negotiations continued in the late 1970s.

Normalisation

One of Nixon's and Kissinger's main aims for *détente* was the **normalisation** of superpower relations. This was achieved, to some extent, by the Basic Principles Agreement and the Helsinki Accords (see pages 62 and 66). Even so, neither of these agreements was comprehensive. The Basic Principles Agreement did nothing to stop superpower conflict in the **Third World** – indeed, Brezhnev hoped that normalisation of the direct relationship between the US and the Soviet Union would allow greater scope for indirect conflict in the Third World. Additionally, neither deal was enforceable.

Trade and economic growth

Both superpowers hoped that *détente* would lead to a reduction of military spending, increased trade between the superpowers, and thus greater economic growth. The first objective was certainly achieved. For example, US defence spending dropped from $406 billion in 1970 to $284 billion in 1976. Trade also increased. Indeed, Soviet imports from the US almost doubled between 1974 and 1975. Nonetheless, economic growth remained slow in the West and the Soviet economy started to shrink. Furthermore, the **Jackson–Vanik Amendment**, passed by Congress in 1974, placed significant restrictions on US-Soviet trade.

The Third World

Détente did nothing to stop superpower competition in the Third World. Indeed, superpower competition was evident in three areas:

- During the Angolan Civil War, which broke out in November 1975, Cuban troops, backed by the Soviet Union, supported the socialist **MPLA** against a **CIA**-backed Western style group. US President **Gerald Ford** failed to get Congressional support for significant US intervention as, after Vietnam, Americans were wary of getting involved in another war against communism. Consequently, communist troops in Angola were successful.

- After the success of communist forces in Angola, the Soviet Union began to support the **left-wing** regime in Ethiopia, sponsoring direct involvement by Cuban forces.

- Finally, in 1979 a communist government came to power in Nicaragua, a country that the US believed to be firmly within its **sphere of influence**.

Communist success in the Third World undermined *détente*. It allowed right-wing politicians in the US to argue that the Soviet Union was taking advantage of the relaxation in US policy to expand its influence.

Support or challenge?

Below is a sample exam-style question which asks how far you agree with a specific statement. Below this is a series of general statements which are relevant to the question. Using your own knowledge and the information on the opposite page decide whether these statements support or challenge the statement in the question and tick the appropriate box.

'*Détente* failed to bring about a relaxation in superpower tensions in the period 1969–1976.' How far do you agree with this view?

	SUPPORT	CHALLENGE
US defence spending dropped from $406 billion in 1970 to $284 billion in 1976.		
Soviet imports from the US almost doubled between 1974 and 1975.		
The Jackson–Vanik Amendment of 1974 placed significant restrictions on US-Soviet trade.		
The Helsinki Accords of 1975 led to the recognition of European borders.		
The Basic Principles Agreement of 1972 recognised the equality of the two superpowers.		
SALT 1 contained an interim agreement on offensive missiles.		
The 1973 oil price shock increased Soviet oil revenues.		

You're the examiner

Below are a sample exam-style question and a paragraph written in answer to this question. Read the paragraph and the mark scheme provided on page 109. Decide which level you would award the paragraph. Write the level below, along with a justification for your choice.

How far do you agree that the oil price shock of 1973 was the main reason for the failure of *détente* in the period 1973–1980?

Although the oil price shock of 1973 played a part in the failure of détente, problems over the SALT 2 negotiations also played a role. The SALT 1 negotiations of 1972 agreed an Anti-Ballistic Missile Treaty, which was very successful. The SALT 2 negotiations were more complicated for various reasons. When Richard Nixon resigned, it was difficult to carry on the negotiations. The Vladivostok Agreement was more successful. Some US Congressmen wanted to stop negotiations with the Soviet Union and to stop détente, and the Germans were worried about arms reduction. Therefore, the oil price shock was only one reason for the failure of détente.

Level: Mark:

Reason for choosing this level and this mark: _____

_____

_____

Jimmy Carter and *détente*

During the mid-1970s, US politicians in both the Republican and Democrat Parties became increasingly critical of *détente*. Specifically, US political leaders were increasingly critical of Soviet human rights violations. Many, including **Theodore Draper**, **George Meany** and Ronald Reagan, felt that the US should use its power to challenge the immorality of Soviet policy, rather than negotiating with an immoral dictatorial regime. **Jimmy Carter** was elected US president in November 1976. Carter's election campaign, which was highly critical of *détente*, reflected these concerns as well as a determination to pursue a more assertive and moral foreign policy.

Carter and arms control

Carter was critical of the SALT 2 negotiations, and in 1977 he proposed much greater cuts than those agreed in Vladivostok in 1974. Soviet leaders did not believe Carter's proposals were serious or realistic.

Negotiations were further undermined by Carter's decision in 1978 to invest in **Trident**, a new generation of nuclear missiles, and to build 23 new missile **silos**. Soviet leaders were perplexed by Carter's contradictory policy of proposing big cuts while simultaneously expanding the US **nuclear arsenal**. Consequently, they found it difficult to trust the new president.

The Vienna Agreement, 1979

In spite of the difficulties between Carter and Brezhnev, the SALT 2 agreement was finally signed in June 1979. Each superpower was to be restricted to 2250 missile launchers. The agreement was reached following Carter's decision to compromise and accept the formula set out in the Vladivostok Agreement. Carter recognised that Soviet negotiators would never accept the radical cuts he had proposed and therefore he altered his position in order to achieve a deal.

The Soviet invasion of Afghanistan, 1979

Soviet troops invaded Afghanistan on 27 December 1979. The invasion placed new strains on superpower relations.

Soviet troops invaded in order to support the left-wing government led by Muhammad Taraki. Soviet leaders feared that the government would be overthrown by militant Islamic groups and were concerned that this would encourage rebellion among militant Islamic groups in the Soviet Union. In this sense, Soviet leaders believed that the invasion was a defensive move, designed to protect their interests and security. The US saw things differently, assuming it was the beginning of a Soviet plan to take control of Central Asia, an area rich in oil.

US reaction

Carter was shocked by the invasion, stating that it called *détente* into question. Carter reacted by increasing defence spending by five per cent, and banning grain and technology exports to the Soviet Union. He also announced that the US would boycott the forthcoming Moscow Olympics. In addition, the US sent military aid to the **Mujahedin**, an Islamic group fighting the Soviet-backed regime.

US intervention was broadly successful. It ensured that Soviet forces were tied up in an unwinnable war for much of the 1980s. This drained Soviet resources, and led to widespread criticism of the Soviet regime.

> **Afghanistan and the end of *détente***
>
> The war in Afghanistan indicated that superpower relations had deteriorated. The fact that the superpowers were now involved in a proxy war showed that neither side was committed to maintaining *détente*.

Spectrum of significance

Below are a sample exam-style question and a list of general points which could be used to answer the question. Use your own knowledge and the information on the opposite page to reach a judgement about the importance of these general points to the question posed. Write numbers on the spectrum below to indicate their relative importance. Having done this, write a brief justification of your placement, explaining why some of these factors are more important than others. The resulting diagram could form the basis of an essay plan.

'The foreign policy of President Jimmy Carter was the main cause of the end of *détente*.' How far do you agree with this view?

1. The foreign policy of President Jimmy Carter
2. The Soviet invasion of Afghanistan, 1979
3. SALT 2 negotiations
4. Watergate, 1973
5. The Helsinki Accords, 1975
6. The oil price shock, 1973

← ── →

Very important   Less important

The flaw in the argument   (a)

Below are a sample exam-style question and a conclusion written in answer to this question. The conclusion contains an argument that attempts to answer the question. However, there is a flaw in the argument. Use your knowledge of the topic to identify the flaw in the argument.

'The foreign policy of President Jimmy Carter was the main cause of the end of *détente*.' How far do you agree with this view?

In conclusion, Jimmy Carter's foreign policy was largely responsible for the end of détente because of its wholly anti-communist character. Carter was morally opposed to détente and therefore found it difficult to negotiate SALT 2, objected to Soviet human rights abuses, and overreacted to the Soviet invasion of Afghanistan in 1979. Indeed, the US reaction to the Soviet invasion was the culmination of a consistent anti-Soviet and anti-détente policy, which led to the boycott of the Olympics and support for the Mujahedin.

The end of *détente* – the roots of the Second Cold War

A series of factors led to the end of *détente*.

Suspicion in the US

Critics of *détente* in the US argued that there was a pattern of Soviet **adventurism** in the Third World. They felt that the Soviet Union had consistently used '**client states**', notably Cuba, to replace moderate regimes with radical socialist governments. The Soviet invasion of Afghanistan seemed to prove them right, and drove a wedge between the Soviet leadership and Carter.

Weak leadership

The successes of the early 1970s were brought about by strong leaders who had the authority to tackle difficult issues. However, by the mid-1970s this was no longer the case. In the Soviet Union, Brezhnev's health declined and he was less able to provide a clear lead. In the US, Nixon's resignation following the Watergate Scandal tarnished the US government, leaving President Ford, then Carter, in a weak position. Additionally, there were serious divisions in the Carter administration regarding *détente*. Cyrus Vance, the Secretary of State, was keen to improve relations with the Soviet Union, whilst Zbigniew Brzezinski, the National Security Advisor, advocated confrontation.

Weak leadership contributed to the end of *détente* because neither side was willing or able to take the tough decisions necessary to sustain the policy.

Human rights

During the 1970s senior US politicians in both parties felt that the Soviet Union had failed to honour the agreements made about human rights in Basket 3 of the Helsinki Accords. Consequently, they argued that *détente* was a worthless policy because the Soviet Union was refusing to abide by the terms of recent agreements.

The economic realities of *détente*

The final reason for the breakdown in *détente* was a partial revival in Western economies. *Détente* had appealed to both superpowers when their economies were stagnating. *Détente* allowed the superpowers to spend less on defence, and develop other aspects of their economies. By 1976, the Western economies were showing signs of revival, while the Soviet economy was still in decline. Consequently, from 1976 the US needed *détente* less than the Soviet Union, and without commitment from both sides the policy was unsustainable.

The West

Economic revival in the West was due to:

- technological innovation, particularly the creation of more powerful and faster computers
- the creation of the G7.

The Soviet Union

Economic decline in the Soviet Union was due to:

- the inefficiency of communist economic planning
- bad harvests in the mid-1970s caused by a combination of droughts and early frosts, which forced the Soviet Union to import large quantities of grain from the West
- a Soviet **balance of payments deficit**, facilitated by increased trade with the West
- a rise in interest rates. The balance of payments deficit had forced the Soviet Union to take out loans from Western countries. As interest rates increased, the loans became more expensive to repay.

The rise of the new right

Détente finally ended with the election of Margaret Thatcher in Britain in 1979 and Ronald Reagan in the US in 1980. Both leaders believed that capitalism was superior to communism as it underpinned political freedom and economic growth. They regarded communism as a morally evil system and believed that the West had a moral duty to challenge it. The election of Thatcher and Reagan signalled that the West was no longer prepared to compromise with the Soviet Union, and therefore that *détente* had ended.

RAG – Rate the timeline

Below are a sample exam-style question and a timeline. Read the question, study the timeline and, using three coloured pens, put a Red, Amber or Green star next to the events to show:

Red: Events and policies that have no relevance to the question
Amber: Events and policies that have some significance to the question
Green: Events and policies that are directly relevant to the question

1) How far did *détente* achieve a relaxation of superpower tension in the period 1969–1980?

Now repeat the activity with the following questions:

2) How far was the growing imbalance of economic power between the superpowers the main reason for the end of *détente*?

3) *'Détente* failed to address the prime causes of superpower tension.' How far do you agree with this view?

				Watergate Scandal					Carter initiates		
Richard Nixon becomes US president	Chinese and US ambassadors meet	Henry Kissinger visits China	Nixon visits China	Gerald Ford becomes US president	Vladivostok Agreement	Helsinki Accords		Jimmy Carter becomes US president	the Trident nuclear programme	Vienna Agreement – SALT 2	US boycott of Moscow Olympics
1969	**1970**	**1971**	**1972**	**1973**	**1974**	**1975**	**1976**	**1977**	**1978**	**1979**	**1980**
Sino-Soviet border conflict	Treaty of Moscow		Moscow Summit – SALT 1 and Basic Principles Agreement	OPEC Crisis		Creation of G7				Soviet invasion of Afghanistan	

Recommended reading

Below is a list of suggested further reading on this topic.

- *The Cold War*, chapter 7, Robert J McMahon (2003)
- *The Cold War: Conflict in Europe and Asia*, section 5, Steve Phillips (2001)
- *Détente and the Nixon Doctrine*, chapter 3, Robert S Litwak (1986)

Exam focus

Below is a sample A grade Part (a) essay. Read it and the examiner comments around it.

How far did relations between the superpowers improve in the period 1969 to 1980? (30 marks)

The introduction focuses immediately on the question, and sets out an argument that will be pursued consistently throughout the essay.

The period 1969 to 1975 saw a significant improvement in superpower relations. This détente or relaxation in superpower tensions was clear from the agreements between the superpowers on arms control and on the basic principles governing superpower relations. However, these agreements were not comprehensive, and were not welcomed by hardline anti-communists in the US. Between 1976 and 1980 tensions grew again, often due to conflict over the 'Third World', an area not covered by the early superpower agreements, as expanding Soviet influence in the 'Third World' persuaded hardliners in the US that the Soviet government was taking advantage of détente.

This paragraph supports the overall argument established in the introduction by providing significant detail concerning the period 1969–1972, and the consequences of the agreements reached in that period.

Relations between the superpowers improved to a great extent between 1969 and 1972, particularly in the area of arms control. The achievement of relative nuclear parity in the late 1960s stabilised superpower relations. Additionally, economic problems in the US and the Soviet Union persuaded political leaders that reducing defence spending would free up resources to invest in economic growth. Consequently, both sides were willing to negotiate an arms reduction package. Leaders of the two superpowers agreed the Strategic Arms Limitation Treaty at the Moscow Summit of 1972. The SALT 1 agreement included a commitment to limit the number of missiles and submarine-launched missiles held by the superpowers. The agreement allowed the Soviet Union an advantage in ICBMs, while the US maintained an advantage in shorter-range weapons stationed in Western Europe. SALT 1 also included an Anti-Ballistic Missile Treaty, which limited each superpower to two Anti-Ballistic Missile Shields. Both sides recognised that the arms limitation aspect of the treaty was only a temporary agreement and agreed to continue negotiating in order to agree further arms controls. This clearly established a degree of trust between the superpowers, which was reflected in the reduction of superpower defence budgets. In the US, for example, defence spending fell from $406 billion in 1970 to $284 billion in 1976. The SALT 1 agreement showed that superpower relations improved considerably in the period 1969 to 1972 because by reducing arms and establishing an on-going dialogue about further arms reductions the superpowers established a degree of trust.

Here, the candidate shows a sophisticated understanding of *détente* by using appropriate technical vocabulary. Specifically, the candidate shows an understanding of the concept of 'normalisation'.

The improvement in the relationship brought about by the SALT 1 agreement was underpinned by the Basic Principles Agreement, which was also agreed at the 1972 Moscow Summit. The Agreement was designed to set out a framework for a new, more stable relationship between the superpowers. The Agreement contained twelve principles, which included a commitment by both sides to respect each other as equals, to seek disarmament, to increase trade and to avoid confrontation. Kissinger and Nixon saw that Agreement as the first step towards the normalisation of superpower relations. Normalisation was evident from the increase in trade between the superpowers; indeed in 1974 alone Soviet imports from the US almost doubled. In this way, the Agreement improved superpower relations significantly in the early 1970s as it established, for the first time, a basic framework governing superpower relations.

This paragraph balances the emphasis in the previous paragraph on normalisation.

However, superpower relations never fully normalised. Specifically, superpower relations with 'Third World' countries were not explicitly discussed in the Basic Principles Agreement. As there was no agreement over superpower action in the 'Third World' there was still potential for conflict. Indeed, conflict in the 'Third World' escalated between 1979 and 1980. For example, in 1975, the Soviet Union backed Cuban troops who supported the socialist MPLA during the Angolan Civil War. The Soviet Union also sponsored Cuban troops who supported the left-wing regime in Ethiopia. Additionally, in 1979 a communist government came to power in Nicaragua, a country that the US believed to be firmly within its sphere of influence. On each occasion, US politicians such as Ronald Reagan, who would later become US president, and Congressman Henry 'Scoop' Jackson tried to influence the government to drop the policy of détente and replace it with a more hardline approach. Finally, the Soviet invasion of Afghanistan to support the left-wing government led by Muhammad Taraki persuaded President Jimmy Carter to end détente. Carter signalled the change in policy by announcing a five per cent increase in defence spending, by banning exports of grain and technology to the Soviet Union, and by announcing a US boycott of the 1980 Moscow Olympics.

Broadly, détente significantly improved superpower relations from 1970 to 1974, but tensions, particularly over the 'Third World', led to a re-emergence of conflict by 1980. However, there were issues even at the high point of détente. Right-wing US politicians were highly critical of détente, for two reasons. First, they argued that by reducing military spending the US was allowing the Soviet Union to catch up, and therefore, the US was losing its advantage in the Cold War. Secondly, figures such as Theodore Draper and George Meany argued that the policy of compromise was immoral, as the US had an ethical duty to stand up to communist evil. Draper and Meany were particularly concerned that the Soviet government and its communist allies were violating human rights. These arguments were reflected in Congressional attempts to undermine détente, with policies such as the 1974 Jackson–Vanik Amendment, which placed significant restrictions on US-Soviet trade. Clearly, even in the period 1970 to 1974 there were still tensions in superpower relations because US hardliners could use their power in Congress to undermine the government's attempts to foster détente.

In conclusion, détente did improve superpower relations significantly in the period 1969 to 1974, as the Basic Principles agreement led to a degree of normalisation between the superpowers, and the SALT 1 agreement established a degree of trust, which was reflected in smaller defence budgets. However, there were significant areas such as the 'Third World' that remained outside the framework established at Moscow. Moreover, there were a growing number of hardliners in the US who thought that compromise was both immoral and likely to undermine the US's leading position in the Cold War. Communist intervention in the 'Third World' weakened the trust between the two governments and strengthened the position of hardliners in the US. This led Carter to take a tougher stance against the Soviet Union and, by 1980, following the Soviet invasion of Afghanistan, détente was over. Therefore, in the long run détente did not lead to a significant improvement in superpower relations in the whole period 1969–1980, rather it led to a brief period of relaxation which was not sustained due to the limits of the normalisation that détente was able to achieve.

This paragraph demonstrates a nuanced understanding of *détente* by arguing that even at the highpoint of *détente*, there were significant tensions between the superpowers.

The conclusion summarises the whole essay and justifies the argument that has been advanced throughout.

30/30

This essay achieves full marks because of the sustained analytical argument developed throughout the essay, the extensive range of factors discussed, the level of detail provided, and the nuanced approach to superpower relations evident in the essay.

What makes a good answer?

You have now considered four sample A-grade Part (a) essays (pages 36–37, 46–47, 60–61 and 74–75). Use these essays to make a bullet-pointed list of the characteristics of an A-grade essay. Use this list when planning and writing your own practice exam essays.

Section 6: Why did the Cold War come to an end in the 1980s?

The primacy of economics

Revised

In some respects, the **Cold War** was an economic competition between East and West. Both superpowers:

- needed large military budgets to finance the development and production of arms to compete in the **arms race**
- competed to offer aid to other countries and in so doing win allies.

By the early 1980s it was clear that the **Soviet Union** no longer had the economic power to compete with the US.

Economic performance

During the Cold War the US economy proved more robust than the Soviet economy. At the end of the Second World War the US was the world's largest economy. There were recessions, particularly at the beginning of the 1970s, but these prompted innovation and, in time, renewed growth. Economic freedom, which allowed competition, was the key to the economic resilience of the US. Indeed, in the late 1970s the US economy was larger than the economies in the **Warsaw Pact** put together.

The Soviet **command economy** was created in the 1930s. Immediately following the Second World War it was the fastest growing economy in the world. From the 1930s until the mid-1960s it was able to produce large quantities of raw materials, such as iron, coal and steel.

However, growth of six per cent during the 1960s slowed to two per cent in the 1970s and declined further in the 1980s. Moreover, even at its peak, the Soviet economy had significant weaknesses.

- First, although the Soviet Union could produce large quantities of products, the quality of what was produced was often very low.
- Secondly, the Soviet economy was unable to produce sophisticated consumer goods or high-tech goods.

Historians argue that the Soviet command economy, in which market forces played a very small role, had less incentive to innovate. By the 1970s the Soviet

economy was experiencing a third problem: for the first time since 1945, it was failing to produce large quantities of raw materials.

	Soviet GNP per capita as a percentage of US GNP per capita
1955	26.1%
1970	37.1%
1980	37.0%
1989	30.8%

Reasons for Soviet economic stagnation

- The Soviet Union was subsidising the **Eastern bloc**. This subsidy amounted to $80 billion throughout the 1970s, and created a huge economic strain.
- The Soviet Union limited the availability of high-tech goods such as computers and modems as it feared they might help opposition groups organise against the government. Indeed, in 1985 the Soviet Union produced 8800 computers compared to more than 6 million produced in the US. The absence of high-tech goods made the economy less efficient.
- By the mid-1980s, 25 per cent of Soviet **GNP** was spent on the military. Consequently, there was less money to invest in projects designed to stimulate economic growth.

Key interpretation: the primacy of economics

Some historians have argued that the end of the Cold War was a result of the Soviet Union's worsening economic problems. According to this interpretation Soviet leaders were forced to seek negotiations with the US on arms control as the Soviet economy could not sustain high levels of military spending. These historians claim that the economic weaknesses of the Soviet Union were of more significance than the Soviet leadership, because Soviet economic decline created the context in which Soviet leaders were forced to act.

Below are a sample Part (b) exam-style question and the three sources referred to in the question. In one colour, draw links between the sources to show ways in which they agree about why the Cold War came to an end. In another colour, draw links between the sources to show ways in which they disagree.

Use Sources 1, 2 and 3 and your own knowledge.

To what extent do you agree with the view that the Cold War ended primarily due to the weakness of the Soviet economy?

SOURCE 1

(From Stephen G Brooks and William C Wohlforth, 'Economic Constraints and the End of the Cold War' in Cold War Endgame, *ed. Williams C Wohlforth, published 2003)*

In interviews and in their memoirs senior former Soviet military advisors uniformly cited the burden of military spending as more than the Soviet economy could bear. These officials agreed that the Soviet economy could not bear the Cold War status quo and that the technological gap [with the West] was large and widening. When asked in an interview whether the Soviet Union had to get out of the Cold War, one advisor responded: 'Absolutely … We simply lacked the power to oppose the USA, England, Germany, France and Italy. We had to find an alternative to the arms race.' Soviet decline made the Cold War's ending on US terms the most likely outcome.

SOURCE 2

(From Mark L Haas in The Ideological Origins of Great Power Politics, *1789–1989, published 2007)*

Most scholars, as well as Soviet decision makers, are in agreement that despite the USSR's economic problems in the mid-1980s, the Cold War did not have to end in this decade. According to many accounts, the Soviet Union continued to possess sufficient resources to extend the Cold War into the early twenty-first century. If Soviet conservatives had continued to govern, it is very doubtful that the Cold War would have ended as early and as smoothly as it did. Conversely, even in the absence of the Soviet Union's economic decline, the 'New Thinkers' rejection of traditional Marxist-Leninist beliefs would have led to a substantial decrease in US-Soviet tensions.

SOURCE 3

(From Sean Sheehan in The Cold War, *published 2003)*

The Cold War did not come to an end because one side achieved a decisive military victory. The US did, however, win an important economic victory in that it was more able than the USSR to support the huge cost of conducting the Cold War. From one viewpoint, this proved that an economy like that of the US, based on private ownership and profit, was better than an economy like the Soviet one that was based around state ownership. In the early 1980s, the US set out to weaken the Soviet economy by denying it trade with the West and holding back Western financial credit and new computer technology.

Ronald Reagan: Cold Warrior

Reagan's leadership style

During his first term (1981–1985), **Ronald Reagan** was an uncompromising anti-communist. Reagan began his presidency by emphasising the moral evil of **communism**. In 1983 he famously referred to the Soviet Union as an 'Evil Empire'. He also stressed the importance of restoring US strength and pride.

Reagan's Cold War policy, 1981–1985

Reagan's policies in this period reflected his belief that the US had a moral duty to stand up to communism:

■ He embarked on the largest peacetime military build-up in US history. By 1985, 30 per cent of the **federal** budget was being spent on the military. In particular, there was the development of the **stealth bomber** and the **Trident** missile.

■ The '**Reagan doctrine**' affirmed the US's willingness to assist anti-communist groups in regions where Soviet infiltration had taken place. For example:

 – In Afghanistan, by 1987, the US was providing $687 million of aid to the **Mujahedin** to fight the Soviet-backed Afghan government, by far the largest **covert action** by the US since the Second World War.

 – In Nicaragua, the US gave military aid to the **Contra group** in their bid to remove the **left-wing** government.

 – In Grenada in 1983, the US sent troops to deal with communist groups.

■ In 1984 Reagan launched the **Strategic Defence Initiative (SDI)**. This was a research program for a space-based system of lasers that would intercept and destroy Soviet missiles. In theory, this could protect the US from a retaliatory strike. In this sense, SDI undermined the '**balance of terror**', which had deterred nuclear war (see page 38).

■ The US deployed **Intermediate Range Missiles (IRMs)** in Western Europe to counter the Soviet **SS20s**. This provoked protest groups in Western Europe but emphasised Reagan's tough line and commitment to **NATO**. He established a positive working relationship with the British prime minister Margaret Thatcher and she agreed to the development of US missile sites in the United Kingdom.

■ Reagan restricted trade with the Soviet Union in order to safeguard the US's competitive advantage. In 1981 he restricted Soviet access to US technology designed to find new oil and gas reserves. In 1982 he restricted Soviet access to US oil and gas.

■ Reagan used hardline anti-communist rhetoric, exposing the moral corruption of communist regimes and the Soviet Union's refusal to abide by the terms of Basket 3 of the Helsinki Accords (see page 66).

Key interpretation: triumphalism

Some historians argue that Reagan's policies in his first term were crucial to the end of the Cold War. They claim that he adopted a strategy of identifying and exploiting key Soviet weaknesses. Specifically, they argue that SDI knocked the Soviet Union out of the arms race. SDI required massive military spending and investment in high-tech goods. Moreover, SDI threatened to make nuclear weapons redundant by neutralising them before they reached their targets. The Soviet economy could not provide the financial or technical resources to compete, which forced Gorbachev to negotiate with the US in an attempt to end the arms race.

Additionally, some historians argue that Reagan's uncompromising anti-Soviet rhetoric added a moral dimension to the Cold War. In this sense, **triumphalists** claim that Reagan was the key reason for the end of the Cold War as his approach exposed the economic and moral weaknesses of Soviet communism.

Below are a sample Part (b) exam-style question and the three sources referred to in the question. In one colour, draw links between the sources to show ways in which they agree about Reagan's role in the end of the Cold War. In another colour, draw links between the sources to show ways in which they disagree. Around the edge of the sources, write relevant own knowledge. Again, draw links to show the ways in which this agrees and disagrees with the sources.

Use Sources 1, 2 and 3 and your own knowledge.

How far do you agree with the view that the Cold War came to an end because of Ronald Reagan's uncompromising anti-communism?

SOURCE 1

(From Paul Johnson, 'Europe and the Reagan Years' in Foreign Affairs 68, *published 1988)*

Reagan's rearmament program, accompanied as it was by a boom in the U.S. economy, had a demoralizing effect on the Soviet elite. It seems to have persuaded a significant number of leading Soviet figures that the attempt to out-arm and out-perform the West, at any rate within the limitations of the production system they had inherited, was hopeless. A new way had to be found, and its direction lay in internal reform of a fundamental nature. Thus the concept of perestroika was born, not merely of internal shame and exasperation at empty shops and shabby conditions, but of an external recognition that their chief ideological competitor, under Reagan's leadership, was far more formidable than they had supposed. Without American dynamism in the 1980s it is highly unlikely that the Soviet leadership would have set out on the unknown, risky and potentially disastrous road of reform. As it was, they felt they had no alternative.

SOURCE 2

(From Frances Fitzgerald in Way Out There in the Blue: Reagan, Star Wars and the End of the Cold War, *published 2001)*

The Cold War was over before the American politicians knew it. No one in Washington foresaw the collapse of the Soviet Union. Yet, as soon as the Soviet Union collapsed, politicians began to advance the argument that the Reagan administration had played a major role in its downfall. A parade of former Reagan officials came forward to assert that Reagan had known all the time that the Soviet Union was on its last legs and had aggressively foreclosed Soviet military options while pushing the Soviet economy to the breaking point. According to these officials, the combination of military and ideological pressures gave the Soviets little choice but to abandon expansionism abroad and repression at home. However, there is little evidence to support this interpretation.

SOURCE 3

(From Norman A Graebener, Richard Dean Burns and Joseph M Siracusa in Reagan, Bush, Gorbachev: Revisiting the End of the Cold War, *published 2008)*

Mikhail Gorbachev broke the Cold War's ideological straitjacket that had prevented Moscow and Washington from resolving their differences. Though politically weakened, Gorbachev conceded nothing to US military superiority. Never did he negotiate from a position of weakness. In doing so, he faced greater political, even physical, risks. After considering all of this, it is difficult to avoid the conclusion that without Gorbachev, the end of the Cold War could have played out very differently.

Mikhail Gorbachev and renewed superpower diplomacy

Mikhail Gorbachev became leader of the Soviet Union in March 1985. He was from a new generation of Soviet politicians. He had a freshness of language and tone that set him apart from previous Soviet leaders. Moreover, unlike his predecessors, he had been influenced by foreign travel, especially in Western Europe.

Gorbachev's 'New Thinking'

Gorbachev introduced a new approach at the top of the Soviet government. His 'New Thinking' included:

Aspect of 'New Thinking'	Policy details
Perestroika	Gorbachev realised that improved living standards for the Soviet people depended on restructuring the economy. The reduction of military spending was central to Perestroika. He argued that economic revival required a massive cut in military spending which in turn required an end to the arms race (see page 78).
Glasnost	He believed that there must be greater freedom of expression and openness in Soviet politics.
Superpower relations	He wanted to pursue a foreign policy based on co-operation rather than confrontation. Specifically he wanted to negotiate an end to the arms race.
Relations with Eastern Europe	Gorbachev indicated there would be no attempt to use military force to assert Soviet control over Eastern Europe. This was in contrast to the Soviet invasions of Hungary in 1956 and Czechoslovakia in 1968 (see pages 30 and 54).

Gorbachev and the future of communism

Gorbachev had no desire to bring Soviet communism to an end. Instead, his reforms were designed to revitalise communism by adapting it to the modern world. As historian Martin Sixsmith argues, 'Gorbachev failed to realise that communism's day was over'. Indeed, Gorbachev hoped that Perestroika would revive the Soviet economy. Similarly, Glasnost was designed to modify the Soviet system, not to transform it. However, reforms created an appetite for further freedom and therefore greater frustration with the Soviet system. The more liberal climate created by Glasnost allowed ethnic national movements to flourish in the **Soviet republics**. It provided an opportunity for ambitious political leaders to capitalise on growing **nationalism** to advance their own careers, by leading **nationalist** opposition groups.

Key interpretation: 'the Gorbachev factor'

Some historians have focused on Gorbachev as the key figure who brought the Cold War to an end. According to this perspective, Gorbachev was significant in two ways. First, his reforms began to acknowledge that Soviet communism had important weaknesses, and that the Soviet Union should learn from the West in terms of political openness and economic competition. In this sense he shifted Soviet policy away from hardline communism and therefore there was increasing common ground between the values of the West and the direction of the Soviet Union. Secondly, some historians credit Gorbachev with opening an arms control dialogue with the West, ending the arms race. In both ways, it can be argued that Gorbachev ended significant aspects of superpower competition.

However, Gorbachev's response to demands for greater political and economic freedom was often contradictory. For example, following a Lithuanian vote in favour of independence from the Soviet Union, Gorbachev authorised a military crackdown in which thirteen people were killed.

Summarise the interpretation

Below are a sample Part (b) exam-style question and the three sources referred to in the question. Each source offers an interpretation of the issue raised by the question. Below each source, summarise the interpretation offered by the source.

Use Sources 1, 2 and 3 and your own knowledge.

How far do you agree with the view that the Cold War came to an end because of the policies of Mikhail Gorbachev?

SOURCE 1

(From Richard Saull in The Cold War and After, *published 2007)*

The Cold War ended because when the ideas and norms that shaped Soviet policy-making were transformed during Gorbachev's leadership – the final phase of de-Stalinisation – these changes were recognised as such and were reciprocated by the West. Thus, where previous Soviet leaders had either been hostile and/or fearful of the West, Gorbachev saw things differently. In particular, he and his colleagues recognised the profound transformation of Western Europe, and Germany in particular, to a stable, liberal state that could not be seen as a threat to Soviet security as it had been in the past. In sum, the Soviet leadership became influenced by liberal political assumptions rather than Marxist-Leninist ones.

SOURCE 2

(From Jonathan Haslam in Russia's Cold War, *published 2011)*

A great deal of debate has revolved around the role of Gorbachev in ending the Cold War. Gorbachev's adversaries in Russia blame him entirely for the destruction of the Soviet Union. Some in the West argue that it was all due to the 'new thinking'. Others argue that Gorbachev as a statesman purposefully brought the conflict to an end. Some argue that Reagan's SDI and military build-up forced Russia off the road. Still more point to the domestic economy, not least the parallel between the falling price for oil on world markets and Russia's overall decline, ensuring the regime's collapse. The history is, as usual, more complicated. Circumstance – domestic and international – and personality both matter.

SOURCE 3

(From Robert McMahon in The Cold War, *published 2003)*

The accession, in March 1985, of Mikhail Gorbachev to the position of leader of the Soviet Union stands as the most crucial turning point in the Cold War's final phase – the one factor, above all others, that hastened the end of the Cold War and the radical transformation in Soviet-American relations that accompanied it. The dynamic, 54-year-old Gorbachev made virtually all of the major concessions that led to landmark arms reduction agreements in the late 1980s. Through a series of wholly unexpected, often unilateral, overtures and concessions, he succeeded in changing the entire tenor of the Soviet-American relationship, in the end depriving the United States of the enemy who it had been seeking to thwart for the past 45 years. Absent this remarkable individual and the astonishing changes of the 1985–90 period become nearly inconceivable.

The moral bankruptcy of Marxism-Leninism

By the late 1970s the Soviet government was experiencing a crisis of legitimacy. In essence, the Soviet people had lost faith in the ideology that underpinned the Soviet regime, and the people of the Eastern bloc resented Soviet domination.

Marxism-Leninism

Marxism-Leninism justified communist rule across the Eastern bloc in two ways.

■ It argued that the Communist Party alone represented the working class.

■ It argued that a '**dictatorship of the proletariat**' was necessary to protect the working class and build a society that was superior to the capitalist societies of the West.

The problems of Marxism-Leninism

During the Brezhnev period (1964–1982) it became increasingly clear that the Communist Party had failed to represent the working class, and failed to create a society that was better than the West.

■ Communist parties tended to be corrupt, and members ruled in order to preserve their own privileges rather than make life better for the workers. For example, in 1970 the average Soviet worker earned 165 roubles a month, whereas members of the Communist Party could earn up to 900 roubles per month.

■ In practice, the 'dictatorship of the proletariat' had created a society that was inferior to Western **capitalism** as it was economically poorer and more politically repressive. Political freedom was extremely limited and, during the Brezhnev era, political opponents were imprisoned in psychiatric institutions. Indeed, the 1977 Soviet Constitution explicitly stated that individual rights were subordinate to the Communist Party. Under Brezhnev, increasing rates of alcoholism, mental illness and suicide clearly indicated that Soviet society was in decline.

Groups such as **Charter 77** and the **Helsinki Watch Committees** argued that the absence of political freedom indicated that Soviet rule was based on oppression rather than consent.

The Eastern bloc

The pattern of corruption, slow economic growth and political repression was true across the whole of the Eastern bloc. Moreover, following the Soviet invasion of Czechoslovakia in 1968 (see page 54) it was clear that governments in the Eastern bloc were subservient to the government of the Soviet Union. Again, this indicated that the communist world was based on repression rather than consent.

> ### Key interpretation: the moral bankruptcy of Marxism-Leninism
>
> Some historians argue that Marxism-Leninism, the ideology on which communism in the Soviet Union and Eastern Europe was based, had become discredited by the late 1980s. It was discredited in the sense that it had failed to deliver the freedom and economic prosperity it had promised. The Communist Party had become a privileged elite with more power and wealth than the workers it claimed to represent.
>
> Furthermore, Gorbachev himself had helped to undermine the legitimacy of communism. As a result of Glasnost, Gorbachev released information concerning the mass murders carried out by communists under Stalin. This provided evidence that the Communist Party was guilty of atrocities and therefore did not have the moral authority to rule.
>
> In these senses there was a growing acceptance that the Communist Party had lost any right it once had to govern. The moral bankruptcy of Marxism-Leninism led to popular pressure to end communist rule in the Soviet Union and across the Eastern bloc.

Contrasting interpretations

Below are three sources offering interpretations regarding why the Cold War came to an end. Identify the interpretation offered in each source and complete the table below, indicating how far the sources agree with each other, and explaining your answer.

	Extent of agreement	Justification
Sources 1 and 2		
Sources 1 and 3		
Sources 2 and 3		

SOURCE 1

(From Daniel Deudney and G John Ikenberry, 'Who Won the Cold War?' in Foreign Policy 87, *published 1992)*

The ideological legitimacy of the Soviet system collapsed in the eyes of its own citizens not because of an assault by Western ex-leftists, but because of the appeal of Western affluence and permissiveness. The puritanical austerity of Bolshevism's 'New Soviet Man' held far less appeal than the 'bourgeois decadence' of the West. For the people of the USSR and Eastern Europe, it was not so much abstract liberal principles but rather the Western way of life that subverted the Soviet vision. Western popular culture – exemplified in rock and roll, television, film, and blue jeans – seduced the communist world far more effectively than ideological sermons by anti-communist activists. As journalist William Echikson noted in 1990, 'instead of listening to Marx and Lenin, generations of would-be communists tuned into the Rolling Stones and the Beatles.'

SOURCE 2

(From Archie Brown, 'The Gorbachev revolution and the end of the Cold War' in The Cambridge History of the Cold War, *eds. Melvyn P Leffler and Odd Arne Westad, published 2010)*

The funeral of the Cold War was a victory for the West in the sense that democratic political systems had proved more attractive to the citizens of Communist Europe than their own political regimes, and market economies had turned out to be more efficient than Soviet-style command economies. This is not at all the same thing as endorsing the popular oversimplification that it was the pressure of the Reagan administration or American military superiority that left the Soviet leadership with no option but to concede defeat. [Indeed] the policy that Gorbachev pursued was one that aroused vast misgivings, and scathing criticism, from a majority of officials within the Soviet government.

SOURCE 3

(From Robert W Sayer in Why did the Soviet Union Collapse?, *published 1998)*

For many people, the impact of glasnost was to erode fatally the sustaining myths of the Soviet regime and to destroy what legitimacy remained to it. It had become painfully obvious that the Soviet Union was nowhere near surpassing the capitalist world and was in fact falling further behind. And while glasnost exposed the country's many problems, it had done little to resolve them. It was equally apparent that the historical foundations of Soviet socialism were built on violence and criminality of monstrous proportions. Ideological alternatives to Marxism-Leninism were out in the open. Now that it was possible to say aloud what many had long believed, the ideological glue of the Soviet Union rapidly dissolved.

The Gorbachev–Reagan thaw

Reagan's attitude toward the Soviet Union changed dramatically during his second term, 1985–1989. In spite of his earlier hardline rhetoric, Reagan was prepared to negotiate with Gorbachev, as he believed that he was serious about reform. As a result the two leaders agreed to convene a series of summits.

The Geneva Summit, 1985

The crucial issue at Geneva was arms control. Gorbachev's key objective was a negotiated end to SDI, as he knew that the Soviet Union had neither the finance nor the technology to compete with the US on a space-based missile shield. Reagan refused to abandon his SDI plans and therefore no agreement was reached. Nonetheless, the meeting established a dialogue between the two leaders and they agreed to meet again with a view to reducing their **nuclear arsenals** by a half.

The Reykjavik Summit, October 1986

Gorbachev opened the summit by proposing the elimination of all nuclear weapons. Again, there was disagreement over SDI. Gorbachev continued to press for its end. Reagan emphasised that SDI was essential to US security. Consequently, the summit ended without agreement. However, it is still regarded as a significant stage in the ending of the Cold War. Significantly, the discussion focused on arms reduction rather than arms limitation. In this sense the negotiations went beyond the SALT agreements of the 1970s (see pages 62 and 68).

Reagan and nuclear weapons

Reagan's long-term goal was to abolish nuclear weapons. SDI was designed, in part, to make nuclear weapons irrelevant. However, in the short term Reagan believed that nuclear weapons were crucial to US security. Therefore, he adopted a policy of expanding the US nuclear arsenal without abandoning hopes of complete disarmament.

Reagan seriously considered Gorbachev's offer of complete **nuclear disarmament** at Reykjavik. However, he was persuaded by Secretary of State George Shultz that Western security depended on a balance of nuclear terror. Therefore, he rejected Gorbachev's proposal.

The INF Treaty, December 1987

Gorbachev and Reagan met for a third time in Washington. Before the summit the Soviet government changed its position on SDI, dropping their demand that the US scrap the programme. Gorbachev had been persuaded by the argument of Soviet scientists, including Andrei Sakharov, that it would be impossible for the US to create an effective nuclear missile shield.

This change of negotiating position led to the agreement of the Intermediate-Range Nuclear Forces (INF) Treaty. The INF Treaty committed the superpowers to remove all intermediate-range missiles – including SS20s, Pershing and Cruise missiles – from Europe.

The Moscow Summit, May 1988

This summit produced no significant progress on nuclear issues but did result in agreements to extend trade and technology links.

Key interpretation: Reagan's negotiating style

Some historians argue that Reagan's willingness to deal with Gorbachev was the key factor that led to the end of the Cold War. They credit Reagan with being willing to negotiate with Gorbachev. This established a dialogue between the two superpowers. Equally, Reagan took Gorbachev's reforms seriously, thus giving Gorbachev's reform agenda credibility in the Soviet government, preventing **hardliners** from blocking important reforms. Finally, Reagan was an idealist and hoped that nuclear weapons could be abolished. Therefore, Reagan took Gorbachev's disarmament suggestions seriously. In this sense, Reagan played a key role in responding to Gorbachev's suggestions and in reciprocating Gorbachev's good faith.

Below is a source providing an interpretation about why the Cold War came to an end. You must read the source, identify the interpretation offered by the source, and use your own knowledge to provide a counter-argument, challenging the interpretation offered by the source.

SOURCE 1

(From Campbell Craig and Fredrik Logevall in America's Cold War: The Politics of Insecurity, *published 2009)*

By the end of Reagan's second term, the Cold War was coming to a peaceful end – the consequence of extraordinary political reforms in Moscow, spectacular political upheaval and boldness in eastern Europe, and, most amazing of all, the establishment of warm relations between the two leaders of the United States and the Soviet Union. With respect to the causes of the Cold War's end, it is fairly clear that the United States played less of a role than did the revolutionary policies undertaken by a new government in Moscow.

Interpretation offered by the source: _____

_____

Counter-argument: _____

_____

_____

○ Write the question   ⓐ

The source above (Source 1) and the following sources relate to key factors in the development of the Cold War. Consider the second historical controversy the exam board specified – Why did the Cold War come to an end in the 1980s? – and review the topics you have revised so far. Having done this, write a Part (b) exam-style question using the sources.

SOURCE 2

(From Beth A Fisher, 'US foreign policy under Reagan and Bush' in The Cambridge History of the Cold War, *eds. Melvyn P Leffler and Odd Arne Westad, published 2010)*

As early as January 1984, the Reagan administration was calling for dialogue, cooperation, and the elimination of nuclear weapons. This was important because these policies created an environment that was receptive to the revolutionary changes that were eventually introduced in Soviet policy. President Reagan played a pivotal role in bringing the Cold War to its conclusion, but not because of his military build-up. Rather, it was Reagan's desire to eliminate nuclear weapons that proved pivotal and provided the crucial signal to Gorbachev that bold initiatives would be reciprocated rather than exploited.

SOURCE 3

(From James Mann in The Rebellion of Ronald Reagan, *published 2009)*

There was nothing in Reagan's first term policies that could induce Gorbachev to abandon the Brezhnev doctrine's assertion of the Soviet Union's right to intervene with force in Eastern Europe. The 'Star Wars' programme did not persuade Gorbachev to sit passively by in 1989 while the Berlin Wall was torn down. It was Reagan's second term policies, his decision to do business with Gorbachev, that set the course for the end of the Cold War. If Reagan had not been responsive then events might have taken a different course during the crucial period from 1985 to 1989. Reagan didn't win the Cold War; Gorbachev abandoned it. By recognising Gorbachev's significance, Reagan helped create the climate in which the Cold War could end.

Use Sources 1, 2 and 3 and your own knowledge.

How far do you agree that _____

_____

Explain your answer, using Sources 1, 2 and 3 and your own knowledge of the issues related to this controversy.

Poland and the 'Sinatra doctrine'

There is general agreement that the collapse of the Eastern bloc was vital to the ending of the Cold War. The disintegration of communism in Europe began with unrest in Poland.

The Polish Crisis, 1980–1981

During the 1970s the Polish economy, like that of the Soviet Union, was in decline. In early 1980 the Polish government responded by raising dramatically the price of consumer goods. Communism in Poland had never enjoyed mass popular support. Moreover, a visit by Pope John Paul II, a Polish national, had stirred the patriotism of Poland's Roman Catholic majority. Against this background, the rise in prices led to massive strikes and, in 1980, the emergence of **Solidarity**, the first free trade union in the Eastern bloc.

Knowing that, under the **Brezhnev doctrine**, he could count on Soviet backing, Poland's communist leader General Jaruzelski established a hardline, military-led communist government, which instituted **martial law** in order to suppress the strikes. Events in Poland showed that, in the early 1980s, the Soviet Union retained a tight grip on Eastern Europe.

The 'Sinatra doctrine'

However, in the later 1980s, Soviet policy towards the Eastern bloc changed. Gorbachev was instrumental in bringing about this change. In December 1988 he publicly abandoned the Brezhnev doctrine. His alternative, which was nicknamed the '**Sinatra doctrine**', accepted that countries in the Eastern bloc could act independently, without fearing Soviet invasion. The new doctrine indicated that Gorbachev was prepared to accept change in Eastern Europe. Nonetheless, he had failed to appreciate the fragility of the East European regimes and consequently was shocked by the pace of change. In this sense, historians argue that the 'Sinatra doctrine' brought about the end of the Eastern bloc. However, this had never been Gorbachev's intention.

The Polish revolution, 1989

During the 1980s Poland's economy failed to revive. Indeed, Soviet-authorised economic reforms led to rapidly rising inflation. As a result, opposition to the Polish communist regime grew. In the late 1980s, knowing that Gorbachev had rejected the Brezhnev doctrine, Jaruzelski abandoned his hardline approach and agreed to multi-party elections. Poland's elections led to the creation of a democratic government led by **Lech Walesa** in 1990.

Key interpretation: the Eastern European revolutions

The Polish revolution inspired revolutions across Eastern Europe. Some historians argue that these revolutions brought about the end of the Cold War. The revolutions, they argue, were a response to the failure of communist economics, and the consequent years of economic hardship. Additionally, the revolutions reflected the fact that people in Eastern Europe had rejected the ideology that underpinned communism. In this sense, communism in Eastern Europe had little popular support and was sustained by the threat of force.

From this point of view, Gorbachev's decision to abandon the Brezhnev doctrine was significant because it removed the threat of force and allowed communism to collapse across Eastern Europe. However, according to this interpretation, Gorbachev was less important than the people of Eastern Europe, as the people of Eastern Europe seized the opportunity to end communism.

SOURCE 1

(From Howard Jones in Crucible of Power: A History of US Foreign Relations Since 1897, *published 2001)*

Gorbachev and others in Moscow recognised the impossibility of holding on to their client states in Eastern Europe, but this reality should not overshadow the long-standing determination of these people to throw off their Soviet captors and achieve independence. Not only did they hate Soviet oppression, but they also despised communism. That archaic system had called for strict one-party rule and the removal of national boundaries, and it ultimately self-destructed in the face of growing popular demands for self-determination. The Communist ideology had proved socially, politically, economically, and morally bankrupt, helping to pull down the entire system from within.

SOURCE 2

(From Campbell Craig and Fredrik Logevall in America's Cold War: The Politics of Insecurity, *published 2009)*

The Cold War ended when it did because Gorbachev decided to withdraw support from the corrupt client states in eastern Europe, because many thousands of eastern Europeans took history into their own hands, and because reformers in the Kremlin saw no alternative than to give up their superpower status peacefully. It is not difficult to understand why some scholars, regarding the five-decade implementation of the Cold War as a great and peaceful victory for the United States, are inclined to give Washington full credit for its termination as well. But the historical record simply does not justify such a conclusion.

SOURCE 3

(From Jussi M Hanhimaki and Odd Arne Westad in The Cold War, *published 2004)*

While general trends condition change, it is people's actions that bring it about. The end of the Cold War was a consequence of the rebellion of those many in Eastern Europe who were tired of economic wants and political oppressions, and who, gradually, came to believe that the Soviet Union under Gorbachev would not act, as the Soviets had done before, to defeat their political demands. The changes started in Poland, where General Jaruzelski's government already in 1988 realised that some kind of settlement with the banned Solidarity trade union movement was a precondition for much-needed Western loans and economic progress.

It was Gorbachev's acceptance of a non-Communist government in Poland that, more than anything, opened the floodgates for political change in Eastern Europe. Just as conflicts over Poland had signalled the beginning of the Cold War system in Europe, the resolution of those conflicts signalled its end.

Margaret Thatcher and Pope John Paul II

British prime minister, Margaret Thatcher, and Pope John Paul II both played a significant role in ending the Cold War.

Margaret Thatcher

Thatcher was an uncompromising anti-communist. Therefore, she supported Reagan's foreign policy. She allowed Reagan to station nuclear missiles in Britain and refused to criticise him for speculating about a 'limited nuclear war in Europe'. Therefore, Thatcher helped Reagan pursue an assertive foreign policy by supporting him and presenting a united front.

Thatcher was also one of the first Western leaders to meet Gorbachev. Her willingness to deal with Gorbachev, summed up in her 1983 comment that 'We can do business together', was one factor that persuaded Reagan to take the new Soviet leader seriously.

Pope John Paul II

Pope John Paul II played a key role in supporting resistance to communism in Poland. As a Polish national, and as head of the Roman Catholic Church, he had enormous moral authority in Poland. His repeated statements in favour of human rights were seen as an implicit challenge to communism. Additionally, his religious statements, such as his prayer that God's Spirit would 'come down and renew the face of the land', were widely interpreted as a call for an end to communism in Poland.

Key interpretation: Margaret Thatcher

Some historians have argued that Thatcher played an important role as an uncompromising supporter of Reagan's foreign policy. Like Reagan, she saw the Cold War in moral terms, viewing communism as an evil that should be resisted.

However, she was also capable of restraint and recognised the mounting pressure on Gorbachev within the Soviet Union. For example, she gave a speech in Kiev, at a time when Ukrainian nationalism was building, avoiding triumphalism and urging caution. Her deep reservations about the rise of a united Germany (see page 90) meant that she played a smaller role in events during 1989.

Key interpretation: John Paul II

Historians have argued that Pope John Paul II played a significant role in challenging the communist government in Poland and therefore played a part in ending the Cold War. The Pope was a passionate believer in the God-given rights of all people. Consequently, he was a consistent supporter of Solidarity. Striking workers used religious imagery as part of their fight against the Polish government. For example, in 1980, they placed a portrait of the Pope on the gates of the Lenin Shipyards in Gdansk. The Pope demonstrated his support for Solidarity by inviting Lech Walesa to the Vatican in 1981.

The Pope was also a Polish national and a figure that united the vast majority of the Polish nation. His three visits to Poland in 1979, 1983 and 1987 demonstrated that he was far more popular than Poland's communist leaders, and inspired Polish Catholics to keep supporting Solidarity. In this sense he undermined the authority of Poland's communist government while conferring the authority of the Church on Solidarity and Walesa.

Write the question

The following sources relate to some of the reasons why the Cold War came to an end in the 1980s. Consider the second historical controversy the exam board specified – Why did the Cold War come to an end in the 1980s? – and review the topics you have revised so far. Having done this, write a Part (b) exam-style question using the sources.

SOURCE 1

(From John Lewis Gaddis in The Cold War, *published 2005)*

When John Paul II kissed the ground at the Warsaw airport on June 2, 1979, he began the process by which communism in Poland – and ultimately everywhere else in Europe – would come to an end. Real power rested, during the final decade of the Cold War, with leaders like John Paul II, whose courage, eloquence, imagination, determination, and faith, allowed them to expose the disparities between what people believed and the systems under which the Cold War had obliged them to live. The gaps were most glaring in the Marxist-Leninist world: so much so that when fully revealed there was no way to close them other than to dismantle communism itself, and therefore end the Cold War.

SOURCE 2

(From Frederic Bozo, Marie-Pierre Rey, N Piers Ludlow and Leopoldo Nuti in Europe and the End of the Cold War: A Reappraisal, *published 2012)*

The evidence does not point to any simple connection between a major European figure and the end of the Cold War. Yet there is little doubt that Margaret Thatcher played her own very special role in the Gorbachev story. It was probably Thatcher who first recognised that Gorbachev was someone with whom the West could do 'business'. It was also Thatcher of all European leaders with whom Gorbachev seemed to enter into the most intense dialogue and discussion after 1985. Indeed, one gets the very clear impression that Gorbachev admired Thatcher a very great deal.

SOURCE 3

(From Jonathan Haslam in Russia's Cold War, *published 2011)*

It is clear that there existed no prior plan of action and that Gorbachev sought to improve the Soviet system, not destroy it. Policy under Gorbachev was improvisational at every stage and dependent on the Western response. In turn, Thatcher's endless berating of Gorbachev and the hard line of the Bush administration when faced with requests for financial aid all played their part in forcing the Soviet leadership to reconsider past policy and move to ever more radical change.

Use Sources 1, 2 and 3 and your own knowledge.

How far do you agree that _____

_____

Explain your answer, using Sources 1, 2 and 3 and your own knowledge of the issues related to this controversy.

The fall of communism in Eastern Europe

Gorbachev's relationship with Eastern Europe

Gorbachev's relationship with Eastern Europe evolved during the late 1980s. In 1989 Gorbachev began to actively encourage democratisation in the Soviet Union's **satellite states**. In addition to Poland there was pressure for reform in Hungary and Czechoslovakia:

- Encouraged by Gorbachev, the Hungarian Communist Party agreed to multi-party elections in 1989. This led to the election of a democratic government in April 1990.
- Czechoslovakia's Civic Forum lead by Václav Havel brought about the '**Velvet Revolution**', leading to the end of communist rule.

Germany

The fall of the Berlin Wall

As communism began to crumble in Eastern Europe, borders with Western European countries began to open. During 1989, thousands of East Germans made the journey via Czechoslovakia to West Germany. This put popular pressure on the East German government to open the border with West Germany. The pressure culminated in the **fall of the Berlin Wall** in November 1989.

German reunification

The fall of the Berlin Wall had raised hopes of a united Germany. However, reunification was problematic for Gorbachev. Hardliners in the Soviet government were concerned:

- It showed a continuing loss of Soviet influence over Eastern Europe.
- A reunified Germany was a potential security threat to the Soviet Union. Hardliners feared that a powerful reunified Germany might want to expand its territory in the east as it had done in 1914 and 1941.

President **George HW Bush** realised that the reunification of Germany had the potential to undermine Gorbachev, leading to his removal from power. Bush believed that the end of the Cold War was dependent on Gorbachev remaining in power. Consequently, he used all of his skills as a negotiator to ensure that the reunification of Germany was not perceived as a threat to the Soviet Union.

Bush met Gorbachev in May 1990 and assured him that, as part of NATO, a reunified Germany would be unable to act unilaterally against the Soviet Union. Germany was unified in October 1990, marking a decisive shift in the balance of power in Europe.

The collapse of the Soviet Union

The Soviet Union comprised fifteen republics. While they were legally independent they were all ruled by the Communist Party, which was led from Moscow. As the Eastern bloc disintegrated, pressure for genuine independence mounted in the majority of the Soviet Union's republics. Gorbachev proposed to replace the Union with a federation in which the fifteen republics would enjoy much greater independence. However, due to the disintegration of the Eastern bloc Gorbachev had little authority within the Soviet government. Consequently, he was unable to create a federation and the Soviet Union officially ceased to exist at the end of 1991.

Key interpretation: the end of the Soviet Union

Historians have argued that the end of the Soviet Union caused the end of the Cold War for a variety of reasons. Some argue that the Cold War was essentially a period of superpower confrontation. The disintegration of the Soviet Union left the US as the world's sole superpower thus ending the Cold War. Others argue that the Cold War was primarily a conflict between two ideologies that were embodied in two political systems. From this point of view, the collapse of the Soviet Union finally proved the superiority of Western capitalism and the failure of Eastern communism, signalling the end of the Cold War.

The fall of communism in the Eastern bloc

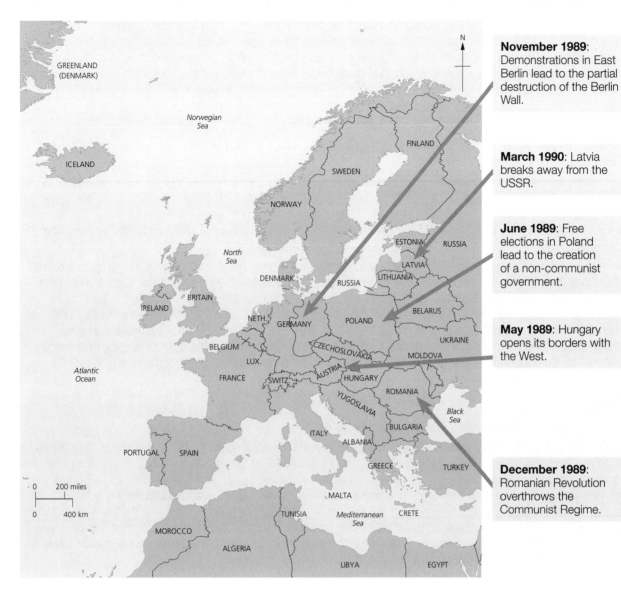

November 1989: Demonstrations in East Berlin lead to the partial destruction of the Berlin Wall.

March 1990: Latvia breaks away from the USSR.

June 1989: Free elections in Poland lead to the creation of a non-communist government.

May 1989: Hungary opens its borders with the West.

December 1989: Romanian Revolution overthrows the Communist Regime.

Add own knowledge

Below are a sample Part (b) exam-style question and the three sources referred to in the question. In one colour, draw links between the sources to show ways in which they agree about the importance of the collapse of communism in Eastern Europe as a cause of the ending of the Cold War. In another colour, draw links between the sources to show ways in which they disagree. Around the edge of the sources, write relevant own knowledge. Again, draw links to show the ways in which this agrees and disagrees with the sources.

Use Sources 1, 2 and 3 and your own knowledge.

How far do you agree with the view that the Cold War came to an end because of the collapse of communism in Eastern Europe?

SOURCE 1

(From Archie Brown, 'The Gorbachev revolution and the end of the Cold War' in The Cambridge History of the Cold War, *eds. Melvyn P Leffler and Odd Arne Westad, published 2010)*

There should be no doubt that one of Gorbachev's principal aims from the outset of his leadership was to end the Cold War. [And] there was a logical connection between Gorbachev's desire to end the Cold War and the subsequent dramatic decision of the Soviet leadership to allow the countries of Eastern Europe to acquire their independence and discard their Communist regimes in the course of 1989. This brought the Cold War, in the sense of military rivalry between two blocs, to an end. The Cold War, as a clash of systems, also ended in 1989, for the changes within the Soviet political system – the development of freedom of speech and contested elections – by then meant that it was no longer meaningful to call the Soviet Union Communist.

SOURCE 2

(From John Lewis Gaddis in The Cold War, *published 2005)*

The upheavals of 1989 caught everyone by surprise. Historians could of course look back and specify causes: resentment over the failure of the command economies to raise living standards; a slow shift in power from the supposedly powerful to the seemingly powerless. What no one understood, at the beginning of 1989, was that the Soviet Union, its empire, its ideology – and therefore the Cold War itself – was a sandpile ready to slide. All it took to make it happen were a few more grains of sand. The people who dropped these grains were not in charge of superpowers or movements or religions: they were ordinary people with simple priorities who saw, seized, and sometimes stumbled into opportunities. The revolution became a triumph of hope. It did so chiefly because Mikhail Gorbachev chose not to act, but rather to be acted upon.

SOURCE 3

(From Beth A Fisher, 'US foreign policy under Reagan and Bush' in The Cambridge History of the Cold War, *eds. Melvyn P Leffler and Odd Arne Westad, published 2010)*

US presidents played a critical role in bringing about the ending of the Cold War. This role, however, was clearly secondary. Reagan became more conciliatory, but Gorbachev revolutionised his country's foreign policy. Bush supported Gorbachev, but his caution paled in comparison to Gorbachev's bold initiatives. The changes in Soviet foreign policy were of a much greater magnitude – and more painful – than were the changes in US policy. The Soviets withdrew from Afghanistan, relinquished their grip on Eastern Europe, reached out to Western Europe, and allowed the emancipation of the Soviet republics. Moreover, Kremlin officials made disproportionate concessions in their quest to end the arms race. While President Reagan and President Bush sought to improve superpower relations, they certainly did not meet Gorbachev halfway.

Recommended reading

Below is a list of suggested further reading on this topic.

- *The Cold War*, chapters 6 and 7, John Gaddis (2005)
- *The Cold War*, chapter 8, Robert J McMahon (2003)
- *America's Cold War: The Politics of Insecurity*, chapters 8 and 9, Campbell Craig and Fredrik Logevall (2009)

Exam focus

On pages 94–95 is a sample answer to the Part (b) exam-style question on this page. Read the answer and the examiner comments around it.

Use Sources 1, 2 and 3 and your own knowledge.

'Gorbachev did more than anyone else to end the Cold War.' How far do you agree with this view?

Explain your answer, using Sources 1, 2 and 3 and your own knowledge of the issues related to this controversy. (40 marks)

SOURCE 1

(From Archie Brown in The Gorbachev Factor, *published 1996)*

There was nothing inevitable either about the timing of the end of the Soviet state or about the way in which, under Gorbachev's leadership, the system was transformed. Taking all his mistakes and some undoubted failures into account, Gorbachev has a strong claim to be regarded as one of the greatest reformers in Russian history and as the individual who made the most profound impact on world history in the second half of the twentieth century. He played the decisive part in allowing the countries of Eastern Europe to become free and independent. Gorbachev did more than anyone else to end the Cold War.

SOURCE 2

(From Kiron K Skinner in Turning Points in Ending the Cold War, *published 2008)*

Throughout the cold war period, Soviet-British relations were full of animosity and tension. Paradoxically, in the second half of the 1980s Britain became the chief promoter of the Soviet Union's positive image in Western Europe. Margaret Thatcher was impressed with Gorbachev's reformist views as early as 1984, even before he became leader of the Soviet Union. Although she never spared sharp criticism of the Communist system, she trusted Gorbachev's commitment to transform the country internally as well as to change its role in the world. Advocating the credibility of the Soviet new thinking, she led the way to its recognition by the Western world and opened a new arena of European politics for the Soviet leader.

SOURCE 3

(From James R Arnold and Roberta Weiner in Cold War, *published 2012)*

As Reagan described it and the scientists conceived it, SDI would employ a number of satellites and space-based radars to destroy warheads in flight. From the perspective of some, particularly the new Soviet leader Mikhail Gorbachev, SDI was a great threat. The Soviet Union lagged behind the United States in computer technology, an area crucial to such an advanced weapons system. The Reagan administration ultimately failed to develop and deploy SDI. Still, the mere threat of SDI put tremendous pressure on the Soviets. Some scholars attribute the Soviet Union's collapse to Reagan's vigorous pursuit of SDI.

The introduction is weak because it does not mention any of the sources and it does not link the quote used in the question to the correct source. Part (b) essays are expected to focus on the interpretation of the sources and therefore the omission of the sources from the introduction suggests a lack of focus.

Gorbachev undoubtedly played a key role in bringing the Cold War to an end. However, although Gorbachev played a key role, he was forced to play the part he did by the profound weaknesses of the Soviet economy, and was facilitated in this by other key figures.

This paragraph clearly focuses on the interpretation in the question. In this sense, it addresses the question immediately, showing excellent focus.

Source 1 credits Gorbachev with having 'a profound impact on world history in the second half of the twentieth century'. It argues that his most significant contribution was his willingness to allow independence for the Eastern bloc. Gorbachev was, as Source 1 argues, a 'reformer'. He renounced the 'Brezhnev doctrine', a doctrine which asserted the Soviet Union's right to intervene in the affairs of another communist nation, in favour of the 'Sinatra doctrine', which asserted that communist countries could follow their own path. This change in policy had a major effect on Eastern Europe. After years of oppression in Poland, Solidarity forced General Jaruzelski to end one-party rule and allow multi-party elections, leading to the election of Lech Walesa in 1990. Indeed, in the late 1980s Gorbachev actively encouraged Eastern bloc countries to embrace multi-party democracy. This led to elections in Hungary in 1989, a 'Velvet Revolution' in Czechoslovakia and finally, the fall of the Berlin Wall. However, Gorbachev's relationship with Eastern Europe was able to change because of better relations between Eastern and Western Europe, and these were brought about, as Source 2 argues, by Thatcher who played a significant role 'advocating the credibility of the Soviet new thinking' to Western Europe's leaders. In this way, while Gorbachev certainly played an important role in dismantling communism in Eastern Europe and therefore ending the Cold War, he was working in a context created by the goodwill of other leaders such as Thatcher.

Here, the candidate shows detailed and focused own knowledge, and links this own knowledge to the sources and to the question.

Moreover, as Source 3 argues, Gorbachev was working within a context of relative weakness. Source 3 argues that 'the Soviet Union lagged behind the US in computer technology, an area crucial to such an advanced weapons system'. Computer technology was only one aspect of Soviet weakness. The Soviet economy, which had been the fastest growing in the world following the Second World War, stagnated in the 1970s and 1980s. Growth rates dropped from an annual average of six per cent in the 1960s to two per cent in the 1970s. Therefore, the Soviet Union was unable to match US military spending. The invasion of Afghanistan also sapped Soviet financial reserves. In this sense Gorbachev was in no position to maintain the 'Brezhnev doctrine', as military intervention in the Eastern bloc would have been costly. More generally, Soviet economic and technological problems meant that Gorbachev had to adopt the reforms mentioned in Sources 1 and 2. Indeed, Source 1 fails to mention that Soviet policy had already changed prior to Glasnost and Perestroika. For example, Brezhnev did not intervene in Poland in 1980 and 1981 as he had done in 1968. Rather he relied on Jaruzelski to crush the rebellion with tacit Soviet support.

In this sense the Brezhnev doctrine was already undergoing some revision under Brezhnev himself. Evidently, Gorbachev's reforms were crucial to bringing the Cold War to an end, but Source 1 is wrong to credit Gorbachev himself with the decisive role because reform had been introduced by his predecessors and because the long-term military, economic and technological decline significantly limited his freedom of action.

Sources 2 and 3 emphasise the importance of other leaders. Source 2 argues that Thatcher 'opened a new arena of European politics' for Gorbachev. Similarly, Source 3 acknowledges that 'some scholars attribute the Soviet Union's collapse to Reagan's vigorous pursuit of SDI'. These two points are clearly related. Reagan perused a policy of negotiation from a position of strength. Therefore he pursued SDI to strengthen the US military position, while meeting Gorbachev at Geneva, Reykjavik and Moscow to find ways of reducing nuclear arsenals. Thatcher adopted a similar approach; as Source 2 argues, 'she never spared sharp criticism of the Communist system', but at the same time, 'she trusted Gorbachev's commitment to transform the country internally as well as to change its role in the world'. In this sense, Thatcher trusted Gorbachev to dismantle the aspects of the Soviet system that were ideologically unacceptable to the West, such as the centralised economy and the lack of individual freedom. Additionally, it seems that the two leaders played complementary roles. As Source 3 argues, Reagan kept the pressure on Gorbachev with SDI, while Thatcher, according to Source 2, worked to open a dialogue between the Soviet leader and the leaders of Western Europe. In this way, Gorbachev certainly played a significant role, but it is difficult to sustain Source 1's interpretation that he played the biggest role, due to the contributions of Reagan and Thatcher.

Overall, Source 1 does indicate that Gorbachev played a key role in bringing about the end of the Cold War. However, Source 2 suggests that Margaret Thatcher also played a role, and Source 3 points to the significance of Ronald Reagan and his vision for SDI as key causes for the end of the Cold War.

This paragraph clearly links aspects of two of the sources. It cross-references the interpretation of Source 2 with the interpretation of Source 3, showing how these interpretations complement each other.

Here the candidate challenges the interpretation of Source 1, using arguments from the other sources and from own knowledge to support this challenge.

The conclusion, like the introduction, is weak. It provides a basic summary of the interpretations of the sources, but does not reach and substantiate an overall judgement.

32/40

This essay is an analytical response integrating own knowledge with the interpretations of the sources. Outside the introduction and conclusion, it develops a sophisticated argument, raising points that clearly support the interpretation in the question, but also showing the importance of the context in which Gorbachev was working. A better introduction and conclusion would have made the argument explicit and therefore allowed the examiner to award a mark in Level 5.

Moving from Level 4 to Level 5

The Exam Focus at the end of Section 1 provided a Level 5 essay. The essay here achieves a Level 4 as the introduction and conclusion are weak. Make a list of the key features of the introduction and conclusion provided in the Section 1 Exam Focus. Rewrite the introduction and conclusion of this essay, ensuring that it reflects the features needed for Level 5.

Timeline

1917	October Revolution in Russia
1918	Outbreak of the Russian Civil War
1919	'Red Scare' in the US
1943	Tehran Conference
1944	Moscow Conference
1945	Yalta Conference
	Harry S Truman becomes US president
	Potsdam Conference – Germany divided and Korea partitioned
1946	Kennan telegram
	Churchill's 'Iron Curtain' speech
	Novikov telegam
1947	Bizonia created
	Truman doctrine
	Marshall Plan
	Communists win elections in Hungary
1948	Communist coup in Czechoslovakia
	Trizonia created
	New currency issued in Western zones of Germany
	Beginning of the Berlin Crisis
	Berlin Airlift
	North and South Korea created
1949	NATO established
	Berlin Crisis ends
	Creation of the Federal Republic of Germany (West Germany)
	Soviet Union tests first atomic bomb
	Mao establishes the People's Republic of China
	Creation of the German Democratic Republic (East Germany)
1950	The China Lobby accuse Truman of 'losing China'
	Sino-Soviet Treaty of Friendship, Alliance and Mutual Assistance
	Outbreak of the Korean War
	UN forces join the Korean War
	Chinese volunteer forces join the Korean War

1952	Mike Tests – US tests its hydrogen bomb
1953	Dwight D Eisenhower becomes US president
	Death of Stalin
	End of the Korean War
1954	Geneva Conference
	First Taiwan Crisis
1955	US deploys B52 Stratofortress
	Nikita Khrushchev emerges as Soviet leader
	Warsaw Pact
	Austrian Treaty – Austria reunited
	Geneva Summit
	Soviet Union tests its hydrogen bomb
1956	Soviet Union deploys TU20 Bear
	Khrushchev's 'Secret Speech'
	Unrest in Poland and Hungary
1957	Soviet Union tests first ICBM
	Second Taiwan Crisis
	Launch of Sputnik 1
1958	Mao launches the Great Leap Forward
	US launch Explorer 1 – first US satellite
1959	Cuban Revolution
1960	Paris Summit
	Khrushchev recalls Soviet advisors from China
	US deploys Polaris submarines
1961	John F Kennedy becomes US president
	US tests the Minuteman ICBM
	Bay of Pigs invasion
	Vienna Summit
	Soviet Union tests Tsar Bomba
1962	Cuban Missile Crisis
1963	Hot line established
	Kennedy visits Berlin
	'Open Letter' published by the Soviet Communist Party
	Nuclear Test Ban Treaty

1964	Khrushchev removed from office		Vienna Agreement – SALT 2
	Leonid Brezhnev emerges as Soviet leader		Soviet Invasion of Afghanistan
	Moscow Meeting	1980	US boycotts Moscow Olympics
1966	Mao launches the Cultural Revolution		Crisis in Poland
1968	Soviet invasion of Czechoslovakia		Establishment of Solidarity
	Brezhnev doctrine	1981	John Paul II invites Lech Walesa to the Vatican
1969	Richard Nixon becomes US president		Ronald Reagan becomes US president
	Sino-Soviet border conflict		Reagan restricts Soviet access to US technology
1970	Chinese and US ambassadors meet	1982	Reagan restricts Soviet access to US oil and gas
	Treaty of Moscow	1983	Reagan's 'Evil Empire' speech
1971	Chinese and US ping-pong teams meet		John Paul II's second visit to Poland
	Henry Kissinger visits China	1984	Reagan launches SDI
1972	Nixon visits China		US deploys Intermediate Range Missiles in Western Europe
	Nixon and Mao issue the Shanghai Communiqué	1985	Mikhail Gorbachev becomes Soviet leader
	Moscow Summit – SALT 1 and Basic Principles Agreement		Geneva Summit
1973	Watergate Scandal	1986	Reykjavik Summit
	Gerald Ford becomes US president	1987	John Paul II's third visit to Poland
	OPEC Crisis		INF Treaty signed
1974	Vladivostok Agreement	1988	Moscow Summit
1975	Helsinki Accords		'Sinatra doctrine'
	Creation of G7	1989	Multi-party elections in Hungary
	Ford visits China		'Velvet Revolution' in Czechoslovakia
1977	Jimmy Carter becomes US president	1990	Germany reunified
1978	Carter initiates the Trident nuclear programme		Lech Walesa elected Polish president
1979	Margaret Thatcher becomes British prime minister	1991	The Soviet Union ceases to exist
	John Paul II's first visit to Poland		

Glossary

38th Parallel The provisional border between North and South Korea agreed in 1945. It ran along the circle of latitude 38 degrees north of the equator.

Adventurism A deliberately risky policy, designed to extend a country's territory or influence, which may well lead to war.

Allies In the context of the Second World War, the US, the Soviet Union and the British Empire.

Andrei Sakharov's Third Idea The Soviet Union's first generation of hydrogen bombs with a megaton yield.

Anti-Ballistic Missile Shields (ABMS) A series of devices – land based, sea based or space based – that are designed to intercept and destroy incoming missiles.

Armistice An agreement to stop fighting.

Arms race A situation in which a number of powers expand their military forces as they compete for dominance.

Atomic bombs The first generation of nuclear weapon: explosive devices based on uranium or plutonium.

Austrian Treaty An international agreement that re-established Austria as an independent state. The state also guaranteed Austria's neutrality in the context of the Cold War.

Axis Powers The military alliance formed by Nazi Germany, Fascist Italy and the Japanese Empire during the Second World War.

Back channel meetings Informal, secret meetings.

Balance of payments deficit A financial situation that arises when the total value of a nation's imports exceeds the total value of its exports.

Balance of terror An international situation in which there is a rough equality of military power between opposing powers. It is often argued that a balance of terror is likely to deter war because the effects of war would be devastating for both sides.

Battlefield tactical nuclear weapons Short-range nuclear weapons, such as artillery shells, torpedoes or even land mines, with a relatively small explosive capacity. They are designed to destroy small targets such as buildings, ships, aeroplanes or tanks.

Bay of Pigs A CIA-backed invasion of Cuba, which took place in April 1961. It failed in its objective of overthrowing Cuba's communist government.

Berlin Wall A barrier constructed by the East German government designed to stop East German citizens travelling to West Germany. It became a symbol of the division of Europe during the Cold War.

Bilateral Agreed by two sides.

Bi-polar world A description of the world that suggests that there are only two real sources of political power. During the Cold War the two superpowers were considered by some historians as the two political 'poles' of world power.

Bomber technology Technology related to large aeroplanes designed to drop bombs.

Bretton Woods Conference Also known as the United Nations Monetary and Financial Conference. Held in 1944, the meeting set up the International Monetary Fund and the World Bank, two organisations that were designed to bring stability to the post-war global economy.

Brezhnev doctrine A statement of Soviet government policy that affirmed the Soviet Union's right to intervene in the affairs of another country in order to protect socialism across the world. In practice, the Brezhnev doctrine justified the Soviet invasion of Czechoslovakia and the overthrow of Czechoslovakia's anti-communist government.

Bureaucrat An official who is responsible for administration within a large company or a government. The term is often used as an insult and in this context it implies someone who spends their time completing pointless tasks that are essentially useless.

Capitalism An economic system based on the private ownership of property, in which goods and services are distributed according to the market.

Cat and mouse relationship A relationship based on unequal power in which the more powerful partner 'toys' maliciously with the less powerful partner.

CENTO A military alliance formed in 1955. The US was not a member of CENTO, but it did promise to provide support to CENTO members in order to stop the spread of communism. CENTO members included Iran, Iraq, Pakistan, Turkey and the British Empire. CENTO was dissolved in 1979.

Charter 77 An informal group of Czech intellectuals who published a manifesto or charter in

January 1977. The charter criticised the Czech government for failing to respect the human rights of Czech citizens.

Chinese Civil War A military conflict between the Chinese nationalists, who officially controlled the government of China, and the Chinese communists lead by Mao Zedong. The conflict began in 1927 and ended in 1949 with the victory of Communist forces throughout mainland China.

Churchill British politician, prime minister and war leader.

CIA The Central Intelligence Agency; the part of the US government responsible for gathering intelligence from other countries.

Client states Countries that are economically, politically or militarily dependent on another more powerful country.

Cold War A conflict between the US and the Soviet Union, starting after the Second World War and ending in the late twentieth century. Although it is described as a 'war', the conflict was mainly ideological and there was never any formal fighting between the two countries.

Comecon The Council for Mutual Economic Assistance; founded in 1949, Comecon was designed to aid economic growth across the Eastern bloc.

Cominform Communist Information Bureau; founded in 1947, Cominform was designed to co-ordinate the communist governments of eastern Europe, bringing them under Soviet control. Cominform was dissolved in 1956 as part of de-Stalinisation.

Command centres Military outposts.

Command economy An economic system in which production is directed centrally by the government. It was designed as a replacement for capitalism.

Communism A political and economic system that emerged in the Soviet Union in the years 1917–1941. It is characterised by single party government and a command economy. Communism as a form of government was established across eastern Europe following the Second World War.

Congress The US Parliament.

Containment A US government policy that aimed to stop the spread of communism.

Contra group Armed rebels who, backed by the US, fought the left-wing Sandinista government in Nicaragua from 1979 to 1990.

Conventional forces Traditional military forces. Conventional forces are typically contrasted with nuclear forces.

Covert action Secret military missions.

Cult of personality The 'cult of personality' was central to Khrushchev's criticism of Stalin's government of the Soviet Union. Khrushchev argued that Stalin had perverted communism by centralising too much power in his own hands, and focusing too much attention on his own achievements. Mao Zedong was also criticised for establishing a personality cult.

Cultural Revolution Also known as the Great Proletarian Cultural Revolution. A period from 1966 until 1976 in which Mao reasserted his authority over the Chinese government by purging rivals from government. During the period 1966–1969, the height of the Revolution, Chinese government became increasingly chaotic as Mao encouraged students and the army to attack the communist government.

Defensive perimeter A geographical area in the Western Pacific in which the US was committed to providing security against communism.

De-Stalinisation A policy introduced after Stalin's death designed to liberalise some aspects of Soviet policy.

Détente A period of decreased tension between the US and the Soviet Union during the Cold War. It is traditionally dated from 1970 to 1980.

Dictatorship of the proletariat According to some communist thinkers, the 'dictatorship of the proletariat' is a historical period in which the working class organises itself to end capitalism and create socialism. Soviet leaders argued that their government was a 'dictatorship of the proletariat'.

Dollar imperialism An interpretation of US foreign policy. Some historians argued that the US used its massive economic power to extend its global power and create an informal empire.

Dwight D Eisenhower Republican president of the US from 1953 to 1961.

Eastern bloc A term used to describe the communist countries of Eastern Europe.

Economic miracle A period of extremely quick economic growth, ending a recession and bringing economic recovery.

Fall of the Berlin Wall The opening and partial destruction of the Berlin Wall that occurred in November 1989.

Federal A term used to describe the central government of the US.

Fidel Castro A Cuban revolutionary and politician, and Cuba's first prime minister following the revolution of 1959.

First World A term used to describe the US and its allies during the Cold War. Also used to refer to highly developed countries.

Freeway A term used to refer to a large road or motorway in the US.

G7 An organisation consisting of the finance ministers from the world's seven most powerful capitalist economies. Formed in 1975, the organisation was designed to facilitate economic co-operation.

GDP Gross Domestic Product: the total wealth produced by a country in a given period.

Geneva Conference of 1954 The Geneva Peace Conference of 1954. Representatives from France and China, alongside nationalists from Vietnam, Cambodia and Laos, attended the conference, which was chaired by Britain and the Soviet Union. The Conference aimed to end the war that was taking place in French Indo China, now Vietnam.

Geopolitical A term that relates to the relationship between political power and geographical territory.

George HW Bush Republican vice president to Ronald Reagan (1981–1989), and president of the US from 1989 until 1993.

George Meany US union leader and head of the American Federation of Labor.

Gerald Ford Republican president of the US from 1973 to 1975. He became president after the resignation of Nixon.

Glasnost The policy of 'openness' introduced by Gorbachev, which allowed access to more information and greater freedom of debate.

GNP Gross National Product: the total wealth produced by a country in a specific period.

Great Depression A period of extreme economic recession, which lasted from 1929 to around 1945.

Great Leap Forward An economic policy introduced by Mao Zedong, designed to lead to massive economic growth in an extremely short space of time. The policy lasted from 1958 to 1961 and led to economic disaster.

Hardliners Essentially, hardliners are unwilling to compromise or negotiate with their Cold War enemies. It is a term that can relate to US or Soviet politicians.

Helsinki Watch Committees Groups set up across the Soviet Union and the Eastern bloc to monitor the extent to which communist governments respected the rights of their citizens. Communist governments had explicitly committed themselves to respect human rights under Basket 3 of the Helsinki Accords. The first Helsinki Watch Committee was established in 1976 in the Soviet Union.

Hydrogen bomb The second generation of nuclear weapon: explosive devices based on fusion technology.

Imperialist To do with a person or a government that supports the policy of pursing the creation and maintenance of an empire. Imperialism also relates to the ideas that might be used to justify such a policy.

Intercontinental Ballistic Missile (ICBM) Long-range missiles capable of striking one continent from another.

Intermediate Range Ballistic Missiles (IRBMs) See: Intermediate Range Missiles.

Intermediate Range Missiles (IRMs) Missiles with a range of 3000 to 5000 km.

Jackson–Vanik Amendment A legal change introduced in 1974 to restrict trade between the US and the Soviet Union.

Jimmy Carter Democrat president of the US from 1975 to 1981.

John F Kennedy Democrat president of the US from 1961 to 1963.

Kremlin The central government district in Moscow, the location of the government of the Soviet Union.

League of Nations An international organisation established following the First World War. The League of Nations was designed to foster international co-operation and world peace. It was dissolved in 1946.

Lech Walesa Leader of Solidarity and first leader of democratic Poland.

Left-wing A term used to refer to people, policies, political groups and government policies that are associated with socialism or communism.

Limited strikes Nuclear attacks that are designed to destroy relatively small areas rather than devastate entire countries.

Manchuria A large region in northeast China, which includes the cities of Shenyang and Harbin.

Manhattan Project A secret military policy commissioned by the US government designed to manufacture nuclear weapons.

Marshal Tito Josip Tito, leader of the communist government of Yugoslavia. Tito successfully resisted Stalin's attempts to control Yugoslavia's government.

Martial law The passing of responsibility for maintaining law and order to the military. Martial law is usually only implemented during times of crisis.

Marxism-Leninism The official ideology of the Soviet Communist Party. It justified communist rule by asserting that the Communist Party was implementing the dictatorship of the proletariat and therefore ruling in the interests of the working class.

Massive retaliation The military strategy favoured by Eisenhower in the event of nuclear war. It entailed responding to any nuclear attack with a counter strike big enough to annihilate the Soviet Union.

Matador missiles The US's first surface-to-surface missile.

Megaton A measure of explosive power, the equivalent to 1000 tons of TNT.

Mike Tests US thermonuclear tests of November 1952. The tests took place on an atoll in the Marshall Islands, which was vaporised by the power of the explosion.

Missile gap The term used in the US for the perceived disparity between the power and size of the Soviet nuclear arsenal compared to that of the US.

Monetary reform In the context of post-war Germany, the term refers to the creation of a new currency.

MPLA People's Movement for the Liberation of Angola: an anti-colonial army and political movement that fought the Portuguese army during the Angolan War of Independence.

Mujahedin The Afghan Mujahedin was a guerrilla movement that believed it was fighting a holy struggle against Soviet forces and the Soviet-backed government of Afghanistan.

Mutually assured destruction (MAD) A military doctrine suggesting that a full-scale exchange of nuclear weapons would result in the complete annihilation of both warring states. MAD suggests that war is unwinnable and therefore undesirable.

Nationalism The belief that all nations have the right to govern themselves. Chauvinistic forms of nationalism tend to emphasise the superiority of one nation.

Nationalist A person, a government, a movement or a policy that supports or advances nationalism.

NATO The North Atlantic Treaty Organisation; founded in 1949, it was designed to provide security for Western Europe during the Cold War.

Normalisation The process of establishing a working relationship between two countries.

North and South Korea In 1945, Korea was temporarily divided between north and south. However, this division soon became permanent. In the late 1940s the Soviet-administered north became an independent communist country, while the US-administered south became an independent capitalist nation.

Nuclear arsenal A stockpile of nuclear weapons.

Nuclear disarmament The abandoning of nuclear weapons.

Nuclear fission A process in which the nucleus of an atom is split. Nuclear fission is essential to atomic bombs.

Nuclear monopoly A situation in which one power alone possesses nuclear weapons.

Nuclear parity A balance between the nuclear military strength of the two sides in the Cold War.

Nuclear umbrella A geographical area that is protected by the nuclear weapons of another state.

OPEC The Organisation of the Petroleum Exporting Countries; an international organisation representing the interests of oil-producing nations, including Iran, Iraq, Kuwait and Saudi Arabia.

Open door policy A policy that affirms that all major powers are allowed access to international markets.

'Open skies' policy The policy of allowing aerial surveillance of missile bases.

Operation Mongoose A series of plots devised by the CIA designed to eliminate Fidel Castro and his regime in Cuba.

Ostpolitik A term that refers to the normalisation of relations between Eastern and Western Europe during the Cold War.

Peaceful coexistence The belief that Soviet foreign policy should be based on the assumption that states with different ideologies could avoid military conflict.

Perestroika The policy of 'restructuring' the Soviet government and economy introduced by Gorbachev. It was designed to revitalise communism by liberalising the state and the economy.

Polish government in exile The Polish government that went into exile after the Nazi invasion of 1939. It went first to France and then in 1940 to London. The US and Great Britain recognised it as the legitimate government of Poland until July 1945.

PRC The People's Republic of China, a communist country founded in 1949.

Proxy wars A conflict in which two or more major powers fight each other indirectly through sponsoring 'proxies', other countries or armed groups.

Quarantine line A naval blockade established during the Cuban Missile Crisis by the US in order to stop Soviet troops or weapons being transported to Cuba.

Quemoy and Matsu Islands in the Taiwan Strait that are not part of the PRC.

Radio Free Europe Also known as Radio Liberty, and funded by the US. The station provided news, information and analysis with a Western slant for audiences in Eastern Europe, Central Asia and the Middle East. Its coverage of the Poznan riots in Poland is said to have inspired the Hungarian rising.

Reagan doctrine The basis of US Cold War strategy from 1981 until 1991. The Reagan doctrine committed the US to providing aid to non-communist forces in the Third World in order to roll back communism.

Realist A politician or statesman who believes that the leaders of all countries tend to pursue self-interest when formulating foreign policy.

Red Scare A period of intense anti-communist paranoia in the early 1920s in the US.

Relative nuclear parity A rough balance between the military strength of the two sides in the Cold War.

Revisionist A term of abuse used by Marxists to indicate that another Marxist has abandoned truly communist policies.

Richard Nixon Republican vice president under Eisenhower (1953–1961), and president of the US from 1969 until 1974.

Right-wing A phrase that describes conservative politicians rather than liberals or socialists.

Robert Kennedy The brother of President John Kennedy. He was involved in back channel negotiations with the Soviet Union during the Cuban Missile Crisis.

Rollback The policy of liberating territory from communist influence.

Ronald Reagan Republican president of the US from 1981 until 1989.

Roosevelt Democratic president of the US from 1933 until 1945.

Russian Civil War A conflict between the Russian communist government and all those who opposed it that ran from 1918 to 1921.

Russian Revolution A political coup that took place in October 1917 that brought the communists to power in Russia.

Satellite states States that are formally independent, but under heavy influence from another state.

SEATO South East Asia Treaty Organisation; SEATO was established by the South East Asia Collective Defence Treaty signed in the Philippines in September 1954. The members of SEATO included Britain and France, who retained colonies in the region. In addition, Australia, New Zealand, Pakistan, the Philippines and Thailand joined the US in signing the Treaty. SEATO members agreed to co-ordinate collective action against communist aggression.

Second World States aligned with the Soviet Union and China.

Silos Underground facilities used to store and launch nuclear missiles.

Sinatra doctrine A phrase that is used to describe Gorbachev's view that Eastern European countries could pursue their own policies. It refers to 'My Way', a song recorded by Frank Sinatra.

Socialism A political philosophy and style of government that aims to create a society that is more equal than capitalist society.

Socialist programme A programme for government that is designed to create a society that is more equal than capitalist society.

Solidarity A trade union established in Poland in 1980.

Soviet republics States such as the Ukrainian Soviet Socialist Republic and the Georgian Soviet Socialist Republic which were part of the Soviet Union.

Soviet revisionism A phrase used by Chinese communist leaders to indicate that Soviet leaders had left the true path to communism.

Soviet Union A group of communist countries dominated by Russia; one of the two superpowers during the Cold War.

Sphere of influence A geographical area in which one country dominates.

Sputnik The first artificial satellite. It was launched by the Soviet Union in 1957. It created fears of a Soviet lead in technology and concerns that the

Soviet Union could develop the capacity to launch missiles from space against any target.

SS20 A medium-range Soviet missile.

Stalinisation The process of establishing Communist rule across Eastern Europe in the late 1940s.

Status quo The current state.

Stealth bomber A military aeroplane which is designed to be difficult to detect by radar.

Strategic Defence Initiative (SDI) Also known as 'Star Wars', SDI was a space-based anti-ballistic missile shield.

Sukarno regime The first independent government of Indonesia, under President Sukarno.

Superpowers A term used to describe the US and the Soviet Union after the Second World War due to their military, economic and political dominance.

Taiwan An island off the Chinese mainland. After the Chinese Revolution of 1949 it remained independent of communist control. Taiwan was the base of the Republic of China, which claimed to be the legitimate government of the whole of China.

Theodore Draper An American historian and political writer who wrote extensively about twentieth-century communism.

Thermo-nuclear devices Hydrogen bombs.

Third World States that were not aligned to either side in the East/West conflict. Often used to refer to undeveloped countries.

Treaty of Moscow An agreement signed by the US, the Soviet Union, as well as East and West Germany. The Treaty formally recognised the division of Germany and committed all of the signatories to work towards the normalisation of relations between East and West Germany.

Trident US submarine-launched ballistic missile developed in the late 1970s.

Triumphalists Historians and politicians who credit the US and Ronald Reagan with 'winning' the Cold War.

Tsar Bomba A Soviet nuclear bomb, the largest ever tested.

U2 A US spy plane.

UN Security Council The part of the UN that is responsible for maintaining world peace. The US and the Soviet Union are both permanent members of the Security Council.

United Nations An international organisation set up in 1945. The United Nations (UN) promotes co-operation between the countries of the world with the aim of ensuring world peace.

Velvet Revolution This phrase describes the peaceful overthrow of communism in Czechoslovakia.

Veto A single vote that has the power to block a policy.

Vietnam War A conflict that took place in East Asia from 1955 until 1975. American troops were sent to fight in Vietnam in large numbers from 1964, although the US had been involved in the war since the 1950s. The American government believed that it needed to send troops in order to stop the spread of communism in Asia.

Warheads The explosive part of a missile.

Warsaw Pact A mutual defence treaty between the eight communist states of Eastern Europe. It was the Soviet Union's response to West Germany joining NATO in 1955. The pact was dissolved in 1991.

Watergate Scandal A major US political scandal that led to the resignation of Richard Nixon as president of the US in August 1974.

Władysław Gomułka The Communist leader of Poland. He was de facto Polish leader from 1945 to 1948, and from 1956 to 1970.

Work quotas The amount of work stipulated by the government that each worker must perform. Work quotas were a feature of some communist regimes.

Yom Kippur War Also known as the 1973 Arab-Israeli War. The War was a conflict between Israel and a coalition of Arab nations that took place in October 1973.

Answers

Page 9, Summarise the interpretation

Source 1 broadly supports the view that the Cold War developed in the years 1945–1953 due to rivalry between the great world powers. The sources argue that the US had the power to negotiate with the Soviet Union, but chose to pursue a more aggressive policy designed to consolidate its status as a great power.

Source 2 argues that Stalin's aggressive attitude towards Poland was unacceptable to the Western allies, and signalled the start of the Cold War. In this sense, Source 2 implies that Stalin's pursuit of policies designed to protect Russia's great power status turned the Grand Alliance into a Cold War.

Source 3 argues that the turning point in superpower relations occurred at the Yalta Conference, which poisoned the relationship between East and West. This source does not explicitly mention great power rivalries.

Page 13, Write the question

How far do you agree that the development of the Cold War between the US and the Soviet Union in the years 1945–1953 was primarily due to the Truman doctrine?

How far do you agree that the US desire to 'restructure the world so that American business could trade, operate, and profit without restrictions' was the main reason for the development of the Cold War between the US and the Soviet Union in the years 1945–1953?

Page 17, Write the question

How far do you agree that 'American demands in Eastern and Central Europe' were the main reason for the development of the Cold War between the US and the Soviet Union in the years 1945–1953?

How far do you agree that the development of the Cold War between the US and the Soviet Union in the years 1945–1953 was primarily due to Stalin's desire to safeguard the security of the Soviet Union?

Page 25, Complete the paragraph

One reason why the Soviet leadership embraced 'peaceful coexistence' in the years following Stalin's death was linked to economic problems within the Soviet Union. For example, **at the heart of Malenkov's 'New Course' was an emphasis on improving the living standards of Soviet people. Malenkov wanted to increase the production of consumer goods by diverting economic resources from arms production. From the mid-1950s, Khrushchev had the same view. Both leaders believed that it would only be safe to reduce Soviet defence spending if the threat of war decreased.** In this way, economic problems within the Soviet Union led Soviet leaders to embrace 'peaceful coexistence' because they hoped that a better relationship with the US would allow them to reduce defence spending and thus improve Soviet living standards.

Page 27, Develop the detail

Eisenhower adopted the 'New Look' in 1953 in part due to concerns about nuclear war.

The 'New Look' changed Truman's policy of limited strikes to a policy of massive retaliation. The limited strikes policy suggested that the US could launch **small numbers of nuclear** weapons against specific targets. **Eisenhower's foreign policy team, including his Secretary of State John Foster Dulles, argued for a change in policy and an increase in the US nuclear arsenal.** Massive retaliation, by contrast, suggested a policy of complete annihilation in response to a nuclear attack **from the Soviet Union. Eisenhower argued, 'We must only plan for total war because it is the only way to preclude any war'.** In this way, one of the reasons why Eisenhower adopted the 'New Look' in 1953 was his concern to prevent nuclear war. Specifically, he adopted the policy of massive retaliation in an attempt to deter Soviet nuclear aggression.

Page 29, Eliminate irrelevance

~~Prior to 1956, Malenkov had pursued the policy of 'peaceful coexistence', signing the Austrian Treaty in 1955 and opening diplomatic channels in order to end the Korean War.~~ Khrushchev's personality meant that he was only partially committed to 'peaceful coexistence' in the period 1956–1961. For example, he was temperamental and unpredictable. He was prone to sudden explosions of anger. He was erratic and rarely consulted colleagues on policy announcements. He was famous for his crudeness and had a tendency to make wild claims about the Soviet Union's nuclear arsenal. Khrushchev's personality undermined 'peaceful coexistence' because he was often aggressive in his dealings with the US. ~~The president of the US at this time was Eisenhower~~ For example the launch of Sputnik 1 in 1957 was an extremely provocative act which destabilised superpower relations. ~~Khrushchev was not the only erratic personality involved in the Cold War. Mao Zedong also initiated rash policies such as the Great Leap Forward.~~ In this way, Khrushchev's erratic personality meant that he was only partially committed to 'peaceful coexistence' because his temperamental behaviour tended to heighten tension between the Soviet Union and the US.

Section 3: The arms race, 1949–1963

Page 39, Eliminate irrelevance

By 1960, there was a balance of terror between the superpowers in terms of hydrogen bombs. The US developed hydrogen bombs in 1952. The 1952 Mike Tests successfully exploded a hydrogen bomb 1000 times as powerful as the one exploded at Hiroshima. Within a year, the Soviet Union had tested its own hydrogen bomb in Kazakhstan. However, the Joe 4 explosion of 12 August 1953 was only 400 kilotons, compared to the Mike Tests, which created a 1-megaton explosion. In this sense, there was an imbalance of power until November 1955, when the Soviet Union tested Andrei Sakharov's Third Idea, creating an explosion as large as the Mike explosion. ~~The balance of terror was a notable feature of the Cold War because the Soviet leadership, which was dominated by Malenkov and Khrushchev, was committed to 'peaceful coexistence'. Therefore, creating a balance of terror was contradictory to Malenkov's 'New Course', which led to the ending of war in Korea and the removal of Soviet military bases in Finland.~~ In this way, by 1960, the development of hydrogen bombs had created a balance of terror as both sides had equal explosive capacity.

Page 43, Develop the detail

One reason why superpower relations reached crisis point over Cuba during 1962 was that the Soviet Union stationed **short-range** nuclear missiles on Cuba. US spy planes spotted Soviet missiles **in September, a month after the warheads began to arrive. US President** Kennedy realised that this increased the Soviet Union's capacity to strike the US, **thus significantly cutting the US advantage in the arms race**. Indeed, Khrushchev planned to send a total of 40 tactical nuclear missiles **and 50,000 Soviet soldiers** to Cuba. As Cuba was not far away from the US **(only 100 miles)**, these missiles endangered most major US cities. In this way, the stationing of Soviet nuclear missiles on Cuba was one reason why superpower relations reached crisis point in 1962 because Kennedy realised that they posed a massive threat to US security, cutting the US advantage in the arms race.

Section 4: Sino-Soviet relations, 1949–1976

Page 49, Eliminate irrelevance

Ideology was one reason for the signing of the Sino-Soviet Treaty of Friendship, Alliance and Mutual Assistance in 1950. Both the Soviet Union and the People's Republic of China were communist powers. ~~North Korea was also a communist power.~~ This meant that they had a common hatred of capitalism, a common desire to spread equality, and a common commitment to economic development through planning. Their mutual commitment to communism meant that they had common enemies in the capitalist world, specifically the US and its ally Britain. ~~This was not the first time that countries had allied due to fear of a common enemy. For example, during the Second World War, Britain, the US and the Soviet Union formed the Grand Alliance in order to combat the Axis Powers.~~ In this way, ideology was one reason for the signing of the Sino-Soviet Treaty because the two sides were united in common objectives and against common enemies.

Page 51, Spot the mistake

The paragraph does not get into Level 4 because although the examples are relevant to the question, their relevance is implicit as there is no explanatory link at the end of the paragraph, linking the examples back to the question.

Page 51, Complete the paragraph

Disagreements between the Soviet Union and China over Taiwan were a further reason for the deterioration of Sino-Soviet relations in the period 1953–1956. For example, **in 1954 Mao launched a military offensive against Taiwan. The US immediately allied with Taiwan, and Mao hoped that China would receive unequivocal military support from the Soviet Union. However, Khrushchev did not want to jeopardise the Soviet policy of 'peaceful coexistence' with the US, and therefore refused to give Mao military back-up. During the 1958 Taiwan Crisis, Mao bombed Quemoy and Matsu in response to the US decision to provide matador missiles to defend Taiwan. Again, Mao hoped for Soviet action, but none was forthcoming.** In this way, tensions over Taiwan were a clear reason for the deterioration of the Sino-Soviet relationship because Mao felt betrayed by Khrushchev and unable to rely on him for further support.

Page 57, Develop the detail

One reason why the US pursued closer relations with China in the period 1969–1970 was the belief that the US and China had areas of common interest. Nixon was aware of the deterioration in Sino-Soviet relations **from 1964 to 1969**. Specifically, he was aware of the recent border conflict **which had taken place over Zhenbao Island in the Ussuri River region,** which had brought the Soviet Union and China to the brink of **nuclear** war. Therefore, Nixon was aware that the two countries shared a common enemy. Nixon hoped that an understanding between the two nations would put the Soviet Union under pressure, **securing China's borders and forcing the Soviet Union to pursue a less aggressive policy against the US in the Cold War**. In this way, a belief in a shared interest between China and the US was one reason why the US pursued closer relations with China because Nixon hoped to exploit common feelings of animosity towards the Soviet Union and turn these to the advantage of the US.

Section 5: *Détente*, 1969–1980

Page 63, Complete the paragraph

Superpower tensions clearly relaxed as a result of the Moscow Summit of 1972. For example, **the summit, the first real success of *détente*, led to two significant agreements. The first concerned nuclear missiles. The SALT 1 agreement committed the superpowers to a temporary agreement on intercontinental ballistic missiles. The Soviet Union gained an advantage in ICBMs, while the US retained its advantage in shorter-range weapons stationed in western Europe. Additionally, the Basic Principles Agreement set out twelve fundamental rules designed to govern superpower relations such as a mutual acceptance of peaceful coexistence and a mutual commitment to seek nuclear disarmament.** In this way, superpower tensions clearly relaxed as a result of the Moscow Summit as it led to arms limitation and a degree of normalisation in superpower relations.

Page 65, Identify an argument

Sample 1 contains the argument.

Page 67, Spot the mistake

The paragraph does not get into Level 4 because it provides a narrative account of the origins of the Helsinki Accords rather than an analytical answer to the question.

Page 67, Eliminate irrelevance

The Helsinki Accords of 1975 certainly helped stabilise superpower relations. ~~The Helsinki Accords were part of a broader policy known as Ostpolitik, which was initiated by the German leader Willy Brandt. Brandt was keen to pursue Ostpolitik because of his commitment to the reunification of Germany.~~ The Helsinki Accords helped stabilise superpower relations by agreeing foundations for three key areas of East–West relations. Basket 1 of the Helsinki Accords agreed borders between East and West, Basket 2 opened the door to more trade, particularly in technology, and Basket 3 contained a commitment to respect human rights. However, the Helsinki Accords did not wholly stabilise superpower relations as US politicians, such as Ronald Reagan, criticised the Soviet Union and the US policy of *détente* by arguing that the Soviet Union and its Eastern European allies were not observing the terms of Basket 3. ~~Reagan later initiated the SDI programme, which some historians believe was crucial in ending the Cold War.~~ In this way, the Helsinki Accords partially stabilised superpower relations by agreeing a framework for East–West relations, but also undermined the stability of superpower relations by allowing right-wing US politicians to criticise *détente*.

Page 69, You're the examiner

The paragraph should be awarded Level 3 because it has a general point that is focused on the question, and attempts analysis in the final sentence. However, the supporting information is only partially relevant and is quite generalised.

Page 71, The flaw in the argument

The argument is flawed because it is based on a sweeping generalisation, namely that the foreign policy of Jimmy Carter was wholly anti-*détente* and anti-Soviet. In reality, Carter's foreign policy was inconsistent and therefore only partially anti-*détente* and anti-Soviet.

Section 6: Why did the Cold War come to an end in the 1980s?

Page 81, Summarise the interpretation

Source 1 supports the view that the Cold War came to an end because of the policies of Mikhail Gorbachev. It argues that Gorbachev's policies transformed the Soviet approach to domestic and foreign policy and therefore allowed a new *dialogue* to open between the Soviet Union and the West.

Source 2 argues that the Cold War ended as a result of a range of factors, including the influence of Gorbachev. In this sense, it *partially* supports the interpretation in the question.

Source 3 argues that the appointment of Gorbachev was 'the most crucial turning point' in the ending of the Cold War as his leadership led to a wholly new relationship between the Soviet Union and the US. Therefore, Source 3 wholly supports the interpretation suggested in the question.

Page 85, Write the question

How far do you agree that 'President Reagan played a pivotal role in bringing the Cold War to its conclusion'?

How far do you agree that 'the United States played less of a role than did the revolutionary policies undertaken by a new government in Moscow' in ending the Cold War?

Page 89, Write the question

How far do you agree that Pope John Paul II played a pivotal role in bringing the Cold War to an end?

How far do you agree that Margaret Thatcher played a pivotal role in bringing the Cold War to an end?

Mark scheme

For some of the activities in the book it will be useful to refer to the mark scheme for the unit. Below and on page 110 is the mark scheme for Unit 3.

Part (a)

Level	Marks	Description
1	1–6	• Lacks focus on the question • Limited factual accuracy • Highly generalised *Level 1 answers are highly simplistic, irrelevant or vague.*
2	7–12	• General points with some focus on the question • Some accurate and relevant supporting evidence *Level 2 answers might tell the story without addressing the question, or address the question without providing supporting examples.*
3	13–18	• General points that focus on the question • Accurate support, but this may be either only partly relevant or lacking detail, or both • Attempted analysis *Level 3 answers attempt to focus on the question, but have significant areas of weakness. For example, the focus on the question may drift, the answer may lack specific examples, or parts of the essay may simply tell the story. Answers that do not deal with factors that are stated in the question cannot achieve higher than Level 3.*
4	19–24	• General points that clearly focus on the question and show understanding of the most important factors involved • Accurate, relevant and detailed supporting evidence • Analysis *Level 4 answers clearly attempt to answer the question and demonstrate a detailed and wide-ranging knowledge of the period studied.*
5	25–30	• As Level 4 • Sustained analysis *Level 5 answers are thorough and detailed. They clearly engage with the question and offer a balanced and carefully reasoned argument, which is sustained throughout the essay.*

Part (b)

A01: Using historical knowledge to form an explanation

*1	1–3	• General points with very limited focus on the question • Inaccurate supporting evidence • No integration of sources and own knowledge
2	4–6	• General points with limited focus on the question • Accurate and relevant – but generalised – supporting evidence • Limited attempts to integrate sources and own knowledge
3	7–10	• General points with focus on the question • Mostly accurate and relevant supporting evidence • Some integration of sources and own knowledge
4	11–13	• General points with strong focus on the question • Accurate and relevant supporting evidence • Integration of sources and own knowledge
5	14–16	• General points with sustained analytical focus on the question • Accurate and well-selected supporting evidence, showing range of knowledge • Full integration of sources and own knowledge

A02: Analysing source material

1	1–4	• Superficial comprehension of the sources • Information from the sources is copied or paraphrased • Extremely limited links between the sources
2	5–9	• Comprehension of some aspects of the sources • Information from the sources is summarised and used to provide a simple answer to the question • Some use of the sources in combination
3	10–14	• The main aspects of the sources are analysed • Evidence from the sources is selected to support and challenge the view expressed in the question • The sources are used in combination
4	15–19	• The sources are interpreted with confidence • The interpretations of the sources are used to debate the view expressed in the question • The sources are used in combination • The essay reaches a judgement based on the interpretations of the sources and own knowledge
5	20–24	• The sources are interpreted with confidence and discrimination • The interpretations of the sources are used to debate the view expressed in the question • The sources are used in combination • The essay reaches a fully substantiated judgement based on the interpretations of the sources and own knowledge